Learning to Love Again

Peter Scariano

PublishAmerica
Baltimore

ISBN: 1-4137-3403-0
PUBLISHED BY PUBLISHAMERICA, LLLP
www.publishamerica.com
Baltimore

Printed in the United States of America

Dedicated to Kathleen,
the mother of my children,
my first true and always love.
And to Jo Anne,
the lady of my dreams,
who taught me to love again.

Acknowledgments

I would like to acknowledge those whose inspiration and support have made this book possible. I wish to thank my wonderful children and their spouses: Mike and Cindy, Jeff and Colleen, Michelle and David, and Chris for their love and understanding throughout this entire healing and growing process. A special thanks to Cathy Baker, whose encouragement was greatly appreciated; to Marsha Georgiopoulos, who has her own story to write some day, and whose suggestions were invaluable; and to Julie Grand whose skills were vital to the completion this book.

Finally, my eternal thanks to Kathy whose spirit compelled me to write this book, and Jo Anne, without whom I would be a hopeless soul.

With Heart So Heavy Laden

My love, deep as any sea,
grows weary in my heart.
I fear that I shall lose it all
as winter's chill cools the hearth.

I have seen fallen leaves
grace eternal mounds,
bitter cold under a blazing sun
as frozen tears hug the ground.

I could not bear the pain again,
and yet, I know we must,
as even the strength of lover's arms
must surely turn to dust.

And with whom eternity spend,
this man who loves the two?
With heart so heavy laden
I commit my love to you.

I

The world seemed a warmer place then. Life was good and even getting better. Our children were nearly grown. Two off to college and another would soon be on her way. Not that we had planned it all that way, but it was working out very nicely. My salary was finally at a point where I didn't need to work summers any longer and, my wife's job was perfect -- close to home, a good salary with excellent benefits and she really enjoyed her work.

We were starting to taste the good life. I had taught for many years. I earned a Master's degree while going to night school and working a part-time job. Kathy had chosen to stay home with the kids until they were old enough for her to seek full-time   employment, and I supported her decision. Now it was all starting to pay off.

The possibilities in our future were a nightly discussion at the dinner table. College visitations were planned with excitement and anticipation. Kathy had not gone to college, as she had helped pay my way through school and keep us afloat during our early years of marriage.

She lived for the days we would go to campus. She obviously enjoyed just being around the college scene and vicariously lived this life through her children. She reveled in it, and her excitement was contagious.

Our twenty fifth wedding anniversary was only two years away. We had made it that far in a world where marriages didn't last nearly so long anymore. We were in love with life and with each other. Then, on what had begun as a glorious Thursday in October, she died.

And with her, every dream I had ever dreamt had just as suddenly died. I felt as if the spark of life itself had been extinguished in me just as it had assuredly been extinguished in her. I had never before felt the inexplicable sting of death and all the horrid, abysmal loneliness it brings. It was a terrible loneliness so deep and disconcerting that I feared I would never see the light of life again. And I didn't care.

People told me it would pass, that time would heal these wounds. But the scars were already much too deep; and my soul was screaming in agony and no one could hear it but me. They all saw the pain in my eyes but they did not understand how deep the pain went. I had never before felt such emptiness and despair. I was surrounded by scores of people whose love, support and compassion to this day I could never repay, yet I was adrift in this sea of humanity and sinking ever deeper and deeper.

You see, Kathy just wasn't the woman I loved; she was the only woman I had ever loved. It was always Kathy and me ever since we had been fourteen years old. We were childhood sweethearts, inseparable in nearly everything we did. We enjoyed each other's company and just knew that that was the way it would always be.

We taught each other about life and love, one learning from the other. We laughed, cried, raised children, and struggled through it all together. We never felt we were doing anything special. There were many others around us doing the same, yet, it was somehow different. I guess just because it was us, as it had always been, as we had always believed it would be. Surely this was not supposed to end so suddenly-without apparent reason, without any goodbyes, without the rest of our lifetimes together.

I had always been so afraid of death, but somehow I convinced myself that Kathy's passing was at least in part a means by which I could prepare myself for my own death. That she, always being the stronger of us two, was again leading the way. But why now, when we were still so much in love and with so much life left to live?

It's funny the last things you remember about someone. I recall sitting in the front seat of my car about to leave for work thinking to myself how much I loved her. Just as I was about to open the car door to tell her so, I saw her robe swinging in the breeze as she turned to re-enter the house. I sat back down in the seat and thought to go after her, but the impulse faded. I have regretted not going to her that morning every day since.

II

After I left Kathy that morning, she would have showered and dressed for the day. She would have finished her cup of coffee and checked all the gas jets on the stove, the door locks and looked around one more time to make sure all was well. Then she would take two aspirin and hope the headache would be gone before she got to work.

These headaches were something she had just gotten used to tolerating. I can't remember a day gone by without her having taken aspirin for a headache. Some years earlier, she had been diagnosed with mild hypertension and was on medication for it. The dosage was very small, but nevertheless she had been taking it for some time. As her headaches became more frequent, she would take more aspirin. I suggested she see her doctor about them, but she knew best and did not see a link between her headaches and the high blood pressure. Actually, about two months before her death, she had told me she was going to quit taking her medication; she felt it was such a small dose, and it didn't warrant the expense.

I recall telling her that that was not a wise decision as I thought she needed to be weaned off the medication. She argued with me, but I made her promise to see a doctor before she did anything like that. She agreed, but reluctantly. To this day I do not know if she actually stopped taking the medication or if she continued to take her daily requirement. After her death I found her prescription bottle in her purse with some pills left. Based on the prescription date, the bottle should have been empty, so I have no idea if she stopped taking the medication. I don't know if in doing so would have had any impact on the rupturing of the aneurism in her brain. What I do know is that if she had gone in for testing, the aneurism would have been detected and it could have been fixed. But how many people would go through the time and expense for something you had no reason to suspect was anything more than just the same old headaches you had had your whole adult life? Kathy didn't. I regret not having been more forceful. One more regret among so many.

She did complain just a week or so before her death that the headaches were becoming more frequent and more severe than usual. She assured me she would see the doctor as soon as it was possible. The irony was that she worked at the local hospital and she knew many of the doctors. But she could be stubborn and if she believed the headaches to be controllable with aspirin, she would not have bothered the doctors with something so minor.

Her drive to the hospital was only five minutes. She would have parked, gone to the coffee shop, bought a cup of decaf with cream and sugar, and walked to her office. Later I was to find out from some of her co-workers that her day was typically uneventful, but she had complained of a nagging headache in the back of her head. More aspirin seemed to curb the pain and reduce it to a dull ache. During the day she would have discussed her hair appointment and the upcoming dinner with our daughter.

Later that afternoon when I spoke with her from work as I did everyday, she asked me if I would be able to join her and our 14-year-old daughter, Michelle, for an early dinner at a local restaurant. I told her I could, as a meeting I was to have attended after school had just been canceled. I was excited about the time the three of us would be sharing. The class bell rang and we hurried our goodbyes without our customary "I love you." That was the last time I was to hear her speak. To this day I cannot recall her voice. And if I could, I don't know if I could stand the pain.

Work for her ended at four o'clock and she went straight to the beauty salon. She was greeted by the girl who always cut her hair. After some small talk, she sat in a chair and tilted her head back to have her hair washed. The beautician recalled the two of them sharing some funny stories.

She asked Kathy to sit up to dry her hair. She placed a towel on Kathy's head and walked her into the main room to cut her hair.

Kathy sat down and the towel was removed. The hairdresser combed her hair back and gently leaned her head forward. She heard a faint gasp as Kathy slumped in the chair.

At first she thought Kathy had fainted and walked around to see if she was all right. As she came around Kathy's slumping body she could see Kathy's eyes rolled back in her head and that she was foaming slightly from the mouth. She called out for assistance. Others helped her gently lay Kathy on the floor, as they were fearful she might fall out of the chair. Then they called 9-1-1.

At 4:15 p.m. I pulled in the driveway and walked eagerly to the front door. I expected to see both my daughter and wife busily doing something together. Instead, I saw Michelle alone in the living room.

"Where's Mom?" I asked, but before she could answer, the phone rang.

"Hello?" I said.

"Are you Kathy's husband?"

"Yes, I am," I responded.

"I'm calling from the beauty salon in town. Your wife is here and has taken ill. The paramedics are with her now," someone said.

"I'll be right there," I said in an urgent manner.

Immediately Michelle recognized from my voice that something was dreadfully wrong. "Dad, what is it?" she asked.

"It's your mother. She…something is wrong. As soon as I find out I'll call you."

"Let me go with you," she pleaded. "Is Mom all right?"

"I don't know right now. But stay here in case she or I may need anything that you will be able to get for us. Okay?"

"Please, call me right away. Please!" she begged.

I hated leaving her alone like that, I didn't know what to expect and I didn't want my daughter to see anything that might scare her even more. I promised I would call her as soon as it was possible.

I can remember thinking many stupid things as I rushed toward the hair salon. I was scared to death. "Maybe she's dead," I thought. There had been no indication of that or of anything serious at all, but I couldn't get that thought out of mind. I was really scared. And I could only think of how scared Michelle was. Then I just dismissed it all as something minor. Something we could all laugh about later over dinner. Certainly it would be nothing that would alter our lives dramatically, certainly not that.

Then I saw the ambulance. Reality reared its ugly head as my heart sank deep into my stomach, and I knew this was something very serious. I was deathly afraid for Kathy, for myself, and everything we knew as us.

As I approached the ambulance, I could see into the main

compartment through what appeared to be a large picture window. I could see my wife, her blouse off, unconscious, lying on a table. There was a mask over her nose and mouth and two people next to her just removing defibrillator paddles from her chest. Her arms were slightly raised at the elbows and both hands were shaking spasmodically outward from her body.

Just then a third paramedic came from around the ambulance and asked me who I was. I explained to him that I was Kathy's husband and asked him what had happened. He told me that they had found her unconscious and were trying to stabilize her now. They were going to transport her to the same hospital she had just left less than thirty minutes before.

When I asked if I could ride with them, he agreed. I jumped in the front seat, and as we pulled away I sat in disbelief. I could not comprehend what exactly was going on, but I knew it wasn't good. No one seemed willing to tell me anything. I wasn't sure why the siren wasn't on. Why were there no flashing lights? They didn't seem to be in a hurry. I didn't like what I was feeling.

As we pulled in to the emergency room drive way I could hear the two paramedics in the back, one male, the other female, laughing loudly. I became infuriated. I screamed at the driver, "What are they laughing at? My wife could be dying back there, and they find something humorous about that?"

The driver was startled; he apologized and said that they were surely laughing about something else. "I don't give a goddamn what they're laughing at. Just tell them to stop."

The ambulance came to an abrupt stop, and I jumped out and ran to the back of the van just as the female paramedic was jumping out.

She told me my wife was fine. "She's stable now," she said. She lied while looking me straight in the eye, never blinking. I knew she was lying and hated her for it. I don't care how long you work around tragedy; there is nothing funny about someone dying. I hated them both for that. I haven't forgiven them yet. I may never.

I sat by Kathy's side in the emergency room while nurses and doctors spoke unconvincing words of hope. I reached over and kissed her cheek and whispered that I loved her. The very words I wished I had said to her when I had last seen her so vibrant with life some ten short hours earlier. As I raised my head from her face, I saw a single tear trickle down her cheek. The only woman I had ever loved was dying.

Later that day I remember asking a friend of mine who is a nurse if that tear was because she was able to hear me or just an anatomical response of some sort.

She said that was all it really was, just some damn response to a death process. To this day I don't believe that at all. Kathy had heard me and was saying good-bye. There isn't a doctor on earth who could prove otherwise to me what I know in my heart to be true. She had said good-bye to me the only way she knew how, in the only way she knew I would understand.

III

Kathy was brought up to intensive care and I was shuffled off to some waiting area near the emergency room. By this time I had arranged a friend of our family to bring Michelle to the hospital. Along with my daughter and me sat a few friends who still held out hope for some sort of miracle that would make this nightmare go away. But about an hour or so later, two doctors came into the room and asked to see me outside in the hallway. Kathy's EEG was flat. There was no chance. No hope. No life.

Later that night, as I sat by Kathy's side in the hospital room waiting for the morning to come, knowing that I had to instruct the doctor to remove her from the respirator, I could only think about how cold she was and how much she hated to be cold. I asked a night nurse to bring some blankets; she came back later with some heated blankets they use in maternity to keep the mothers warm after delivery. It was ironic, I thought, how one of Kathy's fondest memories was how wonderful it felt to be all wrapped up in those blankets after she had delivered her babies, and here she was wrapped in warm blankets to keep her comfortable and safe so she could once again sleep restfully and peacefully.

The blankets were laced with the gentle odor of baby powder, and I thought of the three little children she had brought into this world and whom she had loved more than life itself. My heart cried for them and for all the things they would do without her and all the things she would miss in their lives. I held her hand and prayed for all this to go away, for things to be as they were once before. I squeezed her hand for some kind, any kind, of response, but her hand never moved. I just sat there, blankly staring at her face, with only the rhythmic pattern of the respirator to break the deadly silence of the room.

The next morning, our children and some family friends returned to the hospital.

I asked my children and a personal friend of ours who is a priest if they would want to be with me as Kathy was removed from the respirator. Our oldest son, Michael, and my daughter Michelle, said their goodbyes to their mother and left the room. My son Jeff, Father Tom, two doctors, a nurse and I were there until Kathy's heart stopped beating.

No matter how clinically we as a people elect to define death, the stoppage of a beating heart still symbolizes death in all its finality. It was then that I truly realized that I would never again talk, hold, laugh, cry, argue, sleep, or make love with the only woman I had ever loved. She would never come to see her children grow, mature, succeed in their endeavors. She would never see her children's weddings, or hold her grand children. She would never again smell the flowers in spring or the intoxicating aroma of a camp fire. Yet, she would never grow old before our eyes but rather remain fixed in our memories always as we came to know and love her.

Sometimes the memories of a loved one can haunt us and cause us to deal with pain that was never intended. About a week before Kathy's death she and our oldest son Michael had gotten into an argument over the phone while he was away at school. Later, he would tell me how badly he felt about the incident, even though he had called and apologized to her. What is important is that he does not burden himself with feelings of regret for things he cannot change. His mother loved him, as she did all her children, so deeply that he and his siblings need never worry that they had in any way lost or tarnished that love.

But the burdens we keep with us after others have gone can scar us for life if we let them. Guilt will only diminish an otherwise perfect love. We need only to remember that their love would never have allowed that hurt to go unattended. We would then need to get on with the rest of our lives. Kathy would have expected nothing less from any of us. And to her honor we did that the best we knew how.

The visitation and funeral service is still pretty much a blur to me. We had only a one day visitation yet, the genuine out pouring of love and sympathy shown to me and my family was truly heartwarming. Over a thousand people came to pay their last respects to a woman cut down in the prime of her life. Many people had never even known Kathy, but came to share their sense of loss with me, or our children. I was astounded by this outpouring of love and support, and at times I remember feeling almost removed from it all as the people trickled by in a seemingly endless stream of condolences.

Perhaps what I was most grateful about was that not a single person had said to me that it was her time or that God had a purpose for her in heaven. It seemed as if everyone understood that there was no rationale that would satisfactorily explain why she died. She had an aneurysm in the base of her brain stem, probably from birth, that eventually hemorrhaged and finally ruptured. It caused her cranial cavity to fill with blood, squeezing her brain stem so tightly that even the most basic involuntary processes could no longer sustain life. Medically, I was told she probably had one burning flash at the back of her head as the aneurysm ruptured, and then she fell into unconscious oblivion.

We were fortunate to have had her with us for as long as we did and I am sure she was accepted into the Lord's loving arms when her spirit left this world.

When the church services were over, everyone proceeded to the cemetery. It is a tiny little cemetery in the town Kathy loved. The site is next to a tree and within earshot of a school where children's laughing voices can be heard. It is a place she would have liked and a place where her family can find solace.

After a few brief prayers we were about to leave the cemetery when the priest asked me to look up. There in the sky were three contrails from jets intersecting the space directly above us, an occurrence I had never seen before. He said, "She knows we are here, and she is saying goodbye."

I stared up into the brilliant October sky and didn't know what to think. I turned to Father Tom and said that he was wrong, that it was just coincidence.

He smiled gently at me. I felt in my heart that he was right but I lowered my head and just walked to the car. Contrails or not, Kathy was gone. And I was alone, empty and without feeling.

IV

A life without a love is a terrible life. A life lost of love is not worth living. I lay quietly in my bedroom late that night unable to sleep. My children were out finding solace with their friends. My brother and his wife were downstairs in the living room planning to stay the night just in case someone might need some help or comfort. But by the time my brother would hear and recognize that unmistakable sound of the sliding action of the pump on the shot gun, I would have already loaded one shell and fired.

Nothing had ever been so painfully clear to me in my life. Nothing mattered any more. No person, no thing was of any importance to me. It was simple. My life was over, so why not just end it right here, right now? I never really understood how anyone could take his or her own life. What could possibly be so bad in a life to make a person throw it all away? But you see, that was it, I now understood that one would not be throwing anything away. When you have nothing left there is nothing to lose. It was so simple. I had never felt so un-alive in my life, so empty. I was beyond pain, beyond sorrow. I just didn't want to go on living anymore without Kathy.

I sat up and quietly walked over to the closet in our bedroom and reached for my 12 gauge. As I groped in the darkness for the gun I became confused and angry. It was not there. None of them were there. Someone had taken all my guns. Some goddamn, self righteous, son-of-a-bitch had prevented me from killing myself.

I reached once more in disbelief into the deepest recesses of the closet, and my hand felt the unmistakable cold steel of a barrel.

I calmly walked down the stairs. My brother and his wife sat quietly on the couch reading.

"You took my guns." I stated flatly. "Where are they?"

They turned and stared at each other. Their eyes then focused back toward me. I could tell they both had just realized that their action may well have saved my life.

"They're safe," Barbara said, as she got up from the couch and walked toward the kitchen.

"You missed one," I said.

They were startled, and I could see fear grip their very souls. They thought they had prevented what they feared one of my children or I might do, yet they were aghast that they had missed one of the guns.

"Oh, my God!" Barbara said.

I laughed in relief. I then realized that laughing was an emotion, and I was not yet totally dead inside. The names and faces of our children flashed through my brain. Our children would need me now more than ever. I had nearly thrown it all away. I sat down and cried for the first time since Kathy had died.

V

When she came to see me later in November of that year I was taken by her gentle demeanor. She had a knowledge in her compassionate blue eyes. It seemed to me that she genuinely felt my pain and my sorrow. She explained that she had lost her spouse some five years earlier and I knew she understood.

She walked me through my grief and never let go of my hand. We cried many times together, but she held my spirit up even as my pain surely resurrected her own. She was sent to me, by what power or force I don't know, but I believe it to be true. Jo Anne brought me back from the brink of not caring and taught me to live again.

Three years later, on a sun-drenched Sunday in July, we were joined by family and friends as we began our new life as husband and wife. Together, we were learning to love again.

None of this came easily. Working through all the guilt was the first obstacle, and neither one of us is totally free from that yet. Guilt for being alive while others we have loved are gone. Guilt for finding happiness again in a world that has so many unhappy people. Guilt for so many other reasons and for no reason at all.

Blending families put additional stress on our relationship. And we are still working through that as well. But the most important reason our relationship has been successful is the loving and gentle patience of this wonderful person with whom I have fallen in love.

Jo Anne has had so many hardships to overcome in her own life, yet in spite of these personal burdens and tragedies, she has found time to love me. I am eternally grateful to her. I make it a point before we go to sleep each night to remind her of that, that if I should die in my sleep, I have loved her. I want her never to forget that before I give myself up to the night, she is in my thoughts.

She is the reason for these and other words . . .

You have been the light in my dark storm.
You have listened and understood,
even as my anguish
surely has awakened your own.
You once called me sensitive
but, it is I, who stands in awe of your compassion.

Slowly, as she and I became better acquainted I began to see a lovely, charming, caring and wonderful person all rolled up in one beautiful and humble lady. She is, in many ways, still very much the little girl, which I find to be her most endearing charm.

She has a compassion for all things living and never fails to give me her undivided attention. She makes me feel and still does, that I am the most important thing in her life. I do not know why certain things happen in life. Many people would be grateful for that "*one special* "person in theirs. Many are still searching. I cannot explain why I have been blessed with two such wonderful people in mine. I only know that I once thought love was lost, never to return. And now I find myself in love again.

The human spirit is amazingly resilient. Our need for love is insatiable. Our ability to love and be loved is endless. Where once the pain was so unbearable, it was now tolerable. The darkest despair was now gone with the fresh light of day, for Jo Anne had opened her heart to me and mine was opened to her.

We were both willing to take that chance once more, knowing full well one of us will most likely suffer that pain again. But we both know and understand the risk. Love has no limits; no pain is too great to bear. Love is our greatest strength. It is a tribute to our pasts and a proclamation of our future.

VI

I couldn't believe I was falling in love again. It wasn't possible. So many things were against it, the least of which was what others might think. Oddly enough, we did care what others thought, at least to some extent, but we were more concerned with what our children were thinking. It did matter what they were thinking and we both knew it. If one of our children would have seriously objected to our relationship, it might have ended right then and there. It might have made all the difference. In spite of the fact that we both felt we deserved some happiness again in our lives, our parental instincts would have forced us to put off our relationship until we felt it more appropriate to continue. Undoubtedly, we would have drifted apart, as happens in so many relationships with those pressures, wondering what could have been if only we had persevered the storm of personal needs, fears, jealousies and doubts.

But fortunately our children could see in us a need to be together and the clear and certain strength we drew from each other. Two young families, destroyed by the untimely deaths of spouses and parents, were rising from the ashes of despair and confusion to come together in hope and faith renewed. Not just because we were falling in love, but because our children were also willing to share in our happiness.

And happiness was something Jo Anne had not had for some time.

VII

The water was running in the tub. It was hot. Not scalding, but hot enough to make things right. He emptied the bottle of sleeping pills into his hand and swallowed them down with a mouth full of scotch. He picked up the phone and dialed his home number. He knew she would be there. She was always there when he called. He told her that he loved her and that he was sorry he wasn't the husband she deserved. She was concerned about his tone of voice and felt uneasy about the conversation. She had heard this talk before, but always he had come home. Things were difficult at the office, but surely he would somehow manage to recover from his setbacks. He took pride in overcoming adversity and had done so many times before. Yet, there was a certain finality to his voice this time and it scared her. She asked, but he wouldn't tell her where he was. He assured her that everything would be all right and that he was just tired and needed to rest.

He told her again that he loved her and how much he loved their son, and then hung up the phone. He placed the "Do Not Disturb" sign on the hallway door knob, organized all his letters, turned and walked into the bathroom. He lowered himself into the tub. By this time he was numb enough not to feel the searing heat of the water but rather the embrace of its warm, soothing liquidity. He took another drink, closed his eyes, and the sleep he had so long sought after crept in and took him away.

At ten o'clock the next morning the police came and told her what she had already known. She went to her bedroom, closed the door behind her, and grieved in silence.

VIII

Jo Anne was left alone with a ten year old son, a large home, an aging and demanding mother. She had inherited a business she knew nothing about, social security payments as income, and a modest beneficiary return from her husband's life insurance policy. She was responsible for so much that it sapped her strength away. The struggle between her son's and her mother's needs for her attention often drove her to the brink of exhaustion, but somehow she managed to keep her wits about her. And she dreamed that someone would come to help and love her in a way she had never been helped or loved before.

I never really thought much about fate or destiny. My beliefs in a divine creator hinged on a mixture of Lutheran and Roman Catholic dogma loosely held together by years of confirmation classes and a child's fear of all things evil. As I got older and had my own children, they too were raised in the same tradition, yet I was never convinced it was right or real.

Jo Anne was raised as a Greek Catholic. I'm not really sure what she means by that but her beliefs are similar to mine and so as we have aged we have grown closer to reaching a more comfortable understanding of our place in the universe and in our relationship with God. But there is no question in our minds that we were brought together by forces beyond this world.

Looking back at the way things happened with her marriage, moving to the community in which I taught, losing her husband, struggling for five years, the death of my first wife, teaching Jo Anne's son in my class, my meeting her and she helping me, and I, in turn, helping her seems all too coincidental to us. If I am stretching the concept of fate just a bit, then perhaps you do not believe in fate at all. But I believe God was looking over our shoulders and brought us together, allowing each of us in our own way to fulfill dreams we thought would never come true.

I believe that when a person dies, he or she has the opportunity to help those left behind. That a link exists between this world and the next, and that those who have gone before us can in many ways communicate, either through signs understood by those who would understand, or by interventions of fate. I can offer no proof other than the many occurrences that have happened to me, to Jo Anne, and to our children over these past few years. Perhaps you think I exaggerate, but don't take my word for it. Ask anyone you know who has lost someone dear if what I say is not true. Ask yourself if the same is not true. Perhaps you will come to know this someday yourself. Perhaps you will be the one who intercedes for those who are left behind. Perhaps none of this really happened at all and it is just a figment of someone's imagination.

Yet, I loved, have been loved, and I love again. In any world, I have been blessed.

IX

Jo Anne came to see me for a parent-teacher conference. We discussed her son's progress in my class and I told her that if anything should change in his performance I would call her immediately. As the conference was nearing its end, I could sense she wanted to say something more. She appeared uneasy but began with telling me how sorry she was that I had lost my wife and that she and her son (as did so many other wonderful people from the school district) had attended the visitation service.

I thanked her for her concern and apologized for not having recalled her being there. She said she understood what I was going through, and if I needed to talk she would be willing to listen and share some of her feelings about losing a spouse.

I had forgotten about her husband's death and it struck me as disappointing that I would have forgotten something as important as that. We tend get so wrapped up in our own lives that we often regard the lives of others as being less important or less meaningful than our own. She was still obviously recovering from her own loss, yet she found time to make time for me.

I thanked her again and said if the need to talk with her should arise I would surely feel free to call her. She left with a smile, reassuring me that she meant what she had said. She was offering genuine help, and I was touched by her concern.

To my dismay, her son's efforts in my class were not progressing, and I asked her to come in to discuss the matter again as per her request. We spent the customary twenty minutes or so discussing his work and agreed on some strategies that would hopefully get him back on track. And then the conversation drifted to how I was doing.

I told her that I was fine, but even a blind man could sense my pain. So she politely excused herself. I told her that I would contact her again after the holidays. She told me she would be working with the school chorus over the next couple of weeks in preparation for the Holiday Concert, and that if it was okay, she would stop in from time to time to see how he was doing. I agreed and wished her a Happy Thanksgiving and she hoped mine would be spent with family and friends. I assured her that I would not be alone, but we both knew the upcoming holidays would not be easy.

Thanksgiving came. It was a difficult time for all of us who had known and loved Kathy. It would be my first Thanksgiving without her in nearly thirty years. I was not looking forward to it at all.

When we were all assembled on that day the prayers were again traditionally said by my father. As we held hands around the table laden with traditional fare, I felt as empty as I had ever felt in my life. It was a time of unbelievable pain for all of us. As we offered our thanks for the blessings we had received throughout the year, we couldn't help but feel how this special day was tarnished by the sadness we shared over the loss of one of our own. What was especially difficult for me was how people would deliberately not talk about Kathy's death thinking it would upset me, yet their failure to do so made it seem all the more painful. The fact was my whole world had been brutally torn apart, and I remember that I was mostly thankful for Scotch whiskey that Thanksgiving.

I was especially glad when the day was over. I remember going home and crying and also feeling very guilty as my thoughts would drift to Jo Anne. I wondered if her Thanksgiving had been any better than mine and how she had handled the day.

I hoped it was truly a wonderful day for her and her family. I wish I had been able to talk with her. I wished life was as it had been. I lay in bed, staring at a picture of my wife as I held her pillow, hoping to coax a scent of her from its covering. I did not.

I lay on her side of the bed hoping her spirit would pass through me. It did not.

I was in deep emotional distress. I don't remember falling asleep, but I know it occurred some where between tears and memories.

I was awakened the next morning by the words and music of one of her favorite songs playing on the radio. Another day would begin with tears, another day without her.

X

The Christmas holidays were rapidly approaching. The students were their usual excited selves and of course their excitement was contagious. Periodically throughout those days, as we rapidly approached the seasonal break, I would catch glimpses of Jo Anne in the hallway or in the chorus room playing piano in preparation for the holiday concert. She is a strikingly beautiful lady with long, lean features.

She carries herself very well and I have since learned she prides herself in her posture. I also noticed that on certain occasions when I was noticing her, she was noticing me. Perhaps I was making more of it than there really was. After all, it had been nearly thirty years since I had even thought about another woman in this way. And I wasn't even sure in what way that was. But nonetheless, I felt inexorably drawn to her. She was very beautiful and she had the bluest eyes I had ever seen. I often found myself listening more to the chorus than I had done in the past twenty years.

I was captivated by the accompanist. I found myself walking the hallways more and more during my free periods, hoping to get a glimpse of her, wanting her to know I was there. Wondering if she even knew I was there.

How ironic it seemed to me that here I was in a school, feeling school boyish all over again. But I truly missed the company of a woman. I was feeling a little silly and a lot guilty.

It had been less than three months since my wife had died, and here I was thinking of someone else. I felt a need to talk with Jo Anne, and I felt she had the same need. I wanted her to know that.

Jo Anne would come to see me one more time before the holiday break. I was glad she did. She was wearing a holiday vest with a white blouse. She wore a red and green ribbon in her hair and a pair of stylish jeans that fit her very nicely. She asked how her son was doing, and I told her that he was improving. Then she asked me if I would be attending the concert that night. I said that I had intended to do so and that I looked forward to hearing her play.

She modestly disclaimed any real talent and seemed genuinely glad that I would be attending. I wished her luck and hoped the concert went well.

I do not remember much of the concert that night, but I do recall standing on the side of the gymnasium opposite where she was playing and not being able to take my eyes off her. She looked absolutely beautiful in her red dress, sitting very lady-like at the piano. One time she looked to her left and our eyes met across the sea of heads that separated us. For an instant we were alone in that room. I felt it and I knew she did too. She turned away in that shy little girl way that melts every little boy's heart. It certainly melted mine.

Later that week I would send her a pink poinsettia for the holidays with a card that simply said, "Thinking of you." It was one of the most significant things I had ever done.

XI

My first Christmas without Kathy was at best tolerable and at worse an emotional nightmare. I have always been a strong proponent of tradition, and we had plenty of them. Christmas Eve at the in-laws with dinner, presents, and a visit from Santa Claus. Hurry home to finish last minute wrapping and staying up later than the kids so we could place the gifts under the tree. Finishing the night with a glass of wine wishing we could have given more to the children we so dearly loved. Waking up at the crack of dawn to open presents so eagerly anticipated. Rushing to church, then to the city to celebrate with my family, wondering when all this rushing around would end, but enjoying every minute of it all. Not so unlike the traditions of many other families across this nation and around the world. This year was no different, except for the fact it would be spent without her and it would never be spent with her again. I tried to keep a sense of sanity in all this, but the pain was so deep I didn't really know if it was possible to survive intact.

On one occasion just before Christmas I had been invited to a friend's house in town for a holiday party. There were perhaps a hundred or more people there. I was not feeling very comfortable and was politely pushed in the direction of a lady whom I had known for a few years and who was having marital problems. She was a friend and very kind to myself and family in these early days after Kathy's death. She would often bring

37

food by the house, and we would talk about the way things were and had been and what was to come. After a few drinks, I asked her to attend another party in the area I was planning to attend.

We arrived and everyone was cordial to us, but I became increasingly more and more uncomfortable. She had too much to drink, so we left the party. I suggested we go to a local restaurant for coffee. She was a wonderful lady who was having troubles of her own, but I was not really in a position to help her emotionally or any other way for that matter.

Later that night I felt so very alone. I thought of Kathy and of Jo Anne. I lay awake and wondered what was happening and why I was thinking of someone else.

I felt ashamed and guilty about it all. Later I was to learn that part of feeling that way was one means by which I was accepting Kathy's death and another means by which I was beginning to live without her; a way of re-entering the world of the living. It was a re-awakening to life. I was alive and Kathy was not. I needed to get on with it. My inner need to survive was the driving force behind whatever was to happen.

I was concerned about the appropriate time of mourning; about seeing other women too soon. I didn't know what was or was not too soon. I finally realized that concept was strictly dependent on my comfort level, not on what other people believed to be appropriate or proper. It wasn't like I was out chasing women or anything like that. On the contrary, I had strictly avoided self-help, deceased spouse, or singles groups for fear others would be interested in me or misinterpret my intentions. I didn't really want a relationship. I couldn't afford to be hurt again. I just wanted someone who would take time to understand my feelings without any lasting commitment. But I missed someone to love. I knew if I was to survive intact I would need someone to help me. Someone I could trust and who could trust me. But I also knew that no one would do such a thing without commitment. And I didn't know if I was ready for that yet.

But my thoughts would always go back to Jo Anne. Always back to the lady with the gentle, understanding smile. I would think of her often that holiday season. And I wondered if she thought of me. I wondered if I was out of line by sending her the holiday flower. I hoped I hadn't overstepped the bounds of this newfound friendship. Maybe she would think I was presumptuous. Maybe she was thinking that I was thinking that she was moving too fast. I just wanted her to know how much I was touched by her concern.

And I didn't want her to forget me.

XII

The holidays passed and I managed to survive them. Christmas Eve was especially brutal and New Year's Eve was no treat either. I was alone and lonely.

I missed my wife so very much. I ached for her company and often cried myself to sleep. Thinking of her became an obsession with me. I had never been alone like this before, and I wasn't really sure how I was going to cope, or if I would cope at all. Each day was a struggle and I had a deeper appreciation for what so many single parents must be feeling and dealing with all the time. I was becoming acutely aware of how hard this had to be for a woman in a society where their pay for work done was often not as high as their male counterparts, in a society that didn't understand how hard it was to be a single parent, in a society that seemingly didn't care.

I was beginning to realize that not only had I lost a lifetime partner but also an economic partner whose death meant a difference of nearly $30,000 a year. I had three children. Four years would find two in college at the same time, while all three would be in school for at least one year, possibly two.

I was fearful of many things. I would often get anxiety attacks that left me feeling very much afraid of the future, out of control of the circumstances I found myself in, and helpless to do much about it. The feelings would then subside and I would get back to what I was now accepting as normal until another attack would come. I just assumed these attacks, for lack of a better term, were a fundamental part of the grieving process. I didn't know for sure, but I at least believed that to be true. And I recall that these anxiety attacks were awful. Sometimes I am still fearful that all will not turn out okay.

I would stay up late at night and worry about my children, and I would cry for them and for myself, for what had been, and for what was to come. Fearful that someone might hear my pitiful weeping, I would muffle my cries of anguish, but the pain never seemed to go away. And there was no one to hear my cries for help.

I was alone. I needed someone to help me, and soon, or I would not make the year. I was sinking, and someone needed to throw me a rope. This was not just self pity. I knew what that was, and I had never been that kind of a person. This was sheer distress, simple and pure in its ugliest form.

I tried to appear strong to those around me. I knew they probably saw through my facade, but it didn't matter. I wanted people to see how strong I was and that I didn't need or take help from anyone. I felt so many times that when people would talk to me about Kathy's death and about how things were going that it was more often than not for their benefit rather than my own. I would often console those who attempted to console me.

I had often sought to be alone. Even when I was married, I would seek shelter late at night just by myself to write, listen to music, or sometimes to just sit in the dark. I never really minded being alone, but I did not like loneliness. Loneliness is a slow form of death that saps the strength and spirit of every man or woman. I was never so aware of loneliness as I was those early months following Kathy's death. It was taking its toll on me. I needed something to anchor my life again. More aptly put, I needed someone.

XIII

School resumed after the break. I recall being glad to get back to work. I just wanted to get back to some normalcy again, and coaching basketball would also divert my attention away from the harsh realities of my life. My sons had returned to school and my daughter seemed to be holding her own. Michelle was my greatest concern as she and her mother had been very close, and I knew there were things she would want to talk with her mother about that she would not discuss with me. I would hope that she would feel comfortable doing so, but I knew it wasn't going to happen all the time, so I just resigned myself to that fact and made myself as available as possible to her. I knew we were all going through our own periods of mourning and adjustment and we all needed some space. I believed I gave my children as much space as I could without deserting them and without giving up my own soul. For the most part, we seemed to be adjusting reasonably well. I was encouraged by the strength of my children and felt good they were getting on with their lives.

As I returned to school in early January I found a number of holiday cards in my mail box, many in the handwriting of children. As I proceeded to read them, I came across a card which was clearly written by an adult. I opened it slowly and saw that it was a thank you note. I was being thanked for sending the beautiful poinsettia plant and for thinking enough of her to do such a thing.

Now maybe our relationship would have been the same between us had I not sent her that plant. But to this day I am forever grateful that I did. I believed it would be the key that would open the door between our worlds and allow us the opportunity to step through, if only we were brave enough to enter.

I had this recurring thought that I would live the remaining portion of my life alone. I didn't want to love anyone again. Closer to the truth was the idea that I didn't dare to love again. I was recovering from such a deep loss that I could not and would not think of putting myself in that position once more. But sometimes in life you just believe some things to be true. Maybe you have just a little bit of clairvoyance and you understand some things that defy logic. Well, that's what I felt about Jo Anne.

I knew that she was special in a way that other women would or could not be. There was a near immediate attraction between us. I felt it, and I believed she did too.

Early in January she came to see me at school. It was once again to discuss her son's progress in class. As the conference concluded I asked Jo Anne if she   was seeing anyone on a regular basis. Part of me hoped she would respond with a "Yes." I would have graciously retreated and would have totally understood and hoped she would forgive my presumptuousness. But, I couldn't believe it when she said no. No, she wasn't seeing anyone on a serious basis. I was astounded for a second. How could it be that no one was seeing her regularly? And with as much courage, as I could muster, I asked her perhaps if she would like to have some coffee or dinner after school sometime. She said she would like that. I said, "Great, I'll be in touch soon."

With that she left, and I realized I had perspired right through my shirt. What had I gotten myself into? I couldn't

43

believe I had just asked someone out on a date! I was scared to death but delighted that she said yes. This beautiful lady had said yes, to me!

Later that night I had called some friends who lived in the area. I explained that I was taking a new friend out to dinner and asked if could they recommend a quiet, out-of-the-way restaurant with some atmosphere. Without pressing me too much they made their best recommendation and I believed I was on my way.

The next week I sent a note home with Jo Anne's son suggesting we have dinner on January 29th and if she didn't mind , Chinese at the recommended spot.

A long two days later she responded that the 29th was not possible for her but the 30th would be fine. Chinese would be perfect, but if I didn't mind, her cousin had recommended a different restaurant that was more conducive to conversation.

I wondered what was going on. Was her entire family in on the date? Had I lost control of the situation? I sent another note home with her son (who by now had become a reluctant courier) and agreed to the change in date and restaurant. I suggested 7:00 p.m., and it was done. My first date in nearly twenty five years was about to begin.

XIV

I felt it only appropriate to discuss my upcoming dinner date with my daughter the night before the big event. I had told her that I was staying late after school and would be having dinner with a new friend who had been kind to me and understood what we were going through. Michelle didn't seem surprised. She asked me how we had met and what her name was. I said her name was Jo Anne and that I had met her at school, that she was a parent who had lost her husband some years prior. I really didn't go into anymore detail than that, and I didn't believe there was all that much more to discuss.

I felt badly that I wasn't going to be home for her that next night, but I was really looking forward to the date with Jo Anne. I looked very hard for any signs of disapproval on Michelle's face, but saw none. I saw no unusual body motions. Not even a glint in her eye. I stood there waiting for some kind of inquisition. I didn't really expect this indifference. But then, I really didn't know what to expect.

The next morning I drove Michelle to school, and on the way she asked me when I thought I would be home. I said I didn't think I would be later than ten or so. She smiled and told me to have a good time. She saw the relief on my face and laughed. She told me to relax and enjoy myself. There was a lot of role reversal going on, and we both knew it, we laughed with tears in our eyes. This was not going to be easy for either of us.

That day at school was uneventful, yet there was this nervous anxiety about me. I had a hard time concentrating on my work and wondered if Jo Anne was as jumpy as I was. I doubted it because, being as attractive as I found her to be I was sure had many suitors. I began to get very nervous as school came to a close and even thought about canceling our date. But that would have been the cowardly thing to do and besides, I wanted to see her again. I hung around school and graded papers, prepared the next day's lab work, and still had time to kill. I walked the hallways like a lost puppy waiting for the basketball team to clear out of the locker room so I could shower.

Finally, I showered and shaved and was nervous as hell. I left the building and went to a local floral shop and purchased a single peach-colored rose. It was a beautiful flower, and it reminded me of Jo Anne's gentle and delicate demeanor.

I followed the directions to her home and pulled into her driveway at exactly 7:00 p.m. "Lady in Red," one of the most sensual songs I know, began to play on the radio. I listened for a few seconds and then opened the car door and planted my foot on the drive. I took a deep breath, and with shaky knees walked toward her front door.

I rang the door bell. She was dressed in a red blouse and black skirt and looked absolutely gorgeous. That song kept pounding in my head as I entered her home. Suddenly her dog jumped up on my leg and started barking at me. Jo Anne yelled, "Misty! Get down."

My heart skipped a beat, for just a month before Kathy had died we had put our dog of seventeen years to rest. Her name had been Misty. With "Lady in Red" playing in my head, Jo Anne dressed in scarlet, and dogs named Misty barking in my ear and memory, I felt momentarily adrift in a surrealistic dream. But I was quickly brought back to reality by the staring gaze of Jo Anne's son and her mother, hunched in her chair, as they watched in wide-eyed bewilderment at the carnival before them. I felt sixteen again and on display. Was I good enough for their girl? Did I meet with approval as Grandma checked me over for any visible signs of perversion? And Chris, well, he was just amazed that his teacher was standing in his doorway with a sheepish grin on his face. He loved every minute of it. I was cool, though, as I handed Jo Anne the rose. I could see that she was surprised and genuinely touched by what she later referred to as my thoughtfulness.

Me, I was just glad to be near her once again. She looked stunning in her red blouse, and there was a scent about her that intoxicated me. Whatever it was it very nearly permeated my soul. It was a fragrance I was unaccustomed too, and I was delighted she was wearing it.

She made the obligatory introduction to her mother. Her name was Millie, and she didn't seem as unsocial as Jo Anne led me to believe she could be. I have always been fond of elderly people as I believe they have a different perspective on life experiences that have always interested me. Millie was pleasant and cordial, and I liked her. But things are never as they first seem, and neither are people. Later Millie would prove to be a frightened old lady who saw me as a threat to her security rather than someone who loved her daughter. I would come to know her as a manipulative person; time and disease would cause her to pull her family apart and cost her the respect, if not the love, of her only daughter. But in all fairness, Jo Anne has many fond memories of her mother, especially when they were both much younger and Millie still had her vigor for life. I only wish I had known her then so Jo Anne and I could share such memories.

She invited me into her family room, a great room, beautifully adorned in rich handsome woods. Large, hand-hewn beams from an old barn ran across the ceiling and a large "L" shaped bar made from more of the same timbers comfortably occupied a corner of the room. The most striking feature of the entire "great room" is the huge brick fireplace that encompasses nearly the entire wall opposite the entrance. Your attention is inevitably drawn to the fireplace. It would become for us the center of many a conversation as we learned to know each other.

The fire crackled while just the hint of cherry wood circled the room. We sat by the bar and she asked me if I would like a drink. "Scotch, isn't it?" she asked. I was surprised she knew. She saw a hint of confusion on my face and laughed a bit and said I had joked about it once in a conversation. "I hope that's not a sign of alcoholism?" I sort of asked. She said she didn't really know, but she didn't think so. But it was clear to me that she had been listening to a lot more than I had ever imagined.

We had a few hors d'oeuvres and made some small talk. I complimented her on her appearance and told her that I was just a little nervous. She said she was, too, and that made me feel better. Her son then entered the room, and I was surprised it took him so long to do so. He had a small, rubber basketball in his hands and took a twenty-foot shot at a six-foot tall basketball hoop standing in one of the corners of the room. The ball careened off the backboard and into a plastic window pane that covered a cabinet alongside the fireplace. The sound it made was deafening.

Jo Anne, clearly angered by his lack of manners, snapped at him and asked him to behave.

"I usually make that shot," he said, as he retrieved the ball and prepared for another shot.

I couldn't help but notice the number of these panes around the room that were cracked. "By the looks of it, Chris," I quipped, "I'd say you missed more than you made."

"Come on. Want to play horse?" he asked. Jo Anne reminded him we were going to dinner, and I agreed it was about time to leave.

"Maybe some other time, Chris." I said.

He took a fade-away jumper, and it swished through the hoop. "I woulda' beat ya' anyway," he stated.

Jo Anne apologized for his behavior, and I reassured her it wasn't necessary. It seemed to me that Chris was not the same kid at home that he was at school. But then again, whose kids really were. We left Chris to dream of NBA greatness as we entered a game of our own.

XV

The restaurant was a good choice. It had just the right atmosphere and was not overcrowded. We sat by a window and enjoyed our dinner, and there was never an uncomfortable lull in the conversation. I found Jo Anne to be delightfully reserved. She was deliberate about her choice of words during our conversation and I enjoyed listening to her voice. As could be expected we were both a little guarded, unwilling to expose too much of ourselves on our sleeves. I would come to learn that Jo Anne was particularly concerned about this. She did not want to mislead me in any way or be accused of taking advantage of me, or any man for that matter, who was in a very vulnerable state.

We talked long after the dinner was over. I noticed that we laughed a lot, and I liked it when she smiled.

We talked about our families and about growing up in the city. We discovered that we had gone to neighboring high schools and had frequented the same hot spots. It seemed funny that we had probably crossed paths many times and had never known it. We discovered we liked the same kinds of music and had similar interests in other areas as well.

I couldn't get over how blue her eyes were. I was locked into them. Whenever our eyes would meet, she would shyly look down or away, but they were warm and inviting. I could tell there was a lot going on behind those eyes that remained hidden. But it was getting late, and I had promised Michelle I would be home around ten.

It had been an enjoyable evening, and I didn't want it to end. The ride back to Jo Anne's house was quiet. I was reflecting on the evening and trying to fight off the guilt that I felt surfacing within. Jo Anne, I think, sensed my pensive mood and gave me the space I needed. I pulled into her driveway and walked her to the door. It had been a very nice evening, and I thanked her for making it as easy as it was.

I hugged her and held her tightly for fear I might lose the moment. She hugged me back, and it felt good to be held again. As we parted, I asked her if she might want to have dinner again sometime. She said she would like that.

"By the way," I asked her, "what is that scent you're wearing?"

"Do you like it?" she asked. "It's Oscar de la Renta."

"I like it," I said. "I like it very much."

She thanked me for a lovely evening. I smiled and went back to the car. I turned to see her still standing in the door way. She waved and closed the door slowly behind her.

Her scent, still lingering in the car, kept me company all the way home. I was feeling good, and I decided I would deal with the guilt in the morning.

XVI

The gates to the cemetery were opened. The day was bitterly cold, and the wind howled. Remnants of Christmas wreaths were being tossed about like tumble weeds on the open desert. There was a stark beauty to the scene. It seemed like I was inside an old black and white photograph as I stood by the foot of Kathy's grave waiting for some sign that she understood and would forgive me. I grew angry when none came. " W h a t am I to do?" I asked aloud. "I'm alive!" I cried. "I am sorry you're dead. I had no control over that, and I can't bring you back. If only I could, but I can't."

"Please," I begged, "understand that I need to do this if I am to survive."

The wind only howled louder and the cold stung me to the bone. It was there, standing on the cold and frozen ground, that I came to know the answer I was seeking.

I knew Kathy would want me to find someone else to live my life with, just as I would have wanted her to do the same had it been me who had died. Yet, it was hard, very hard, to think in those terms. It felt like I was betraying her then and sometimes it still does. But I needed to remind myself constantly that it was "til death do us part." I had honored my commitment to Kathy and fulfilled my responsibilities as best I could, given all my human faults and frailties. I did not love her any less because she was gone, nor had I forgotten how much my life had been enriched because of her. She was still in my heart and would always be. Not allowing yourself the opportunity to love again, for fear of betraying a previous love, deprives you of life's most precious gift. Why would I want to do that? And to what honor and memory would this be best served?

.A few days passed by and I was again in emotional turmoil. I wanted to see Jo Anne, but I was still dealing with the guilt from the first date. I was also depressed because I was paying bills. They were getting larger while my income seemed to be seriously shrinking. I had received some insurance money from my wife's policies, but I had already placed much of that money in custodial accounts for my children's educations. If I was going to fail as a single parent, I didn't want that failure to jeopardize their chances for graduation. As I paid the bills my mind drifted back to just a few months before Kathy's death. It was as vivid a memory as was my pain of it.

It had been a social evening at my brother's home. It was just the four of us. We were all laughing. We had just finished one of those games adults play to amuse themselves; as usual, it had been the men against the women. We did this often whenever we got together. But this night would soon turn ugly. For whatever reason, we begin discussing household finances and the expense of raising children and sending them off to college. Kathy remarked how difficult it was to balance the budget and meet all the payments on time. My brother laughed and said paying the bills was not that big a deal, that anyone could pay bills as long as the money was present.

I agreed with him. "It was really no big deal to write a few checks and stick them in the mail," I remarked

It didn't take long to see the hurt in Kathy's eyes, as she was the one in our household who, for whatever reason and for every reason, had assumed this responsibility. I did the best two-step I could do, but the damage had already been done. She fired back, "Why don't *you* pay the bills from now on?"

"It wouldn't be that hard," I responded. "Besides, what could it possibly take to figure it out?"

"What would you do if I were to die tomorrow?" she asked. "You have no idea which bill is due when, or about any of our finances for that matter."

She had me by the short hairs because I really didn't know. I just brought home a check and deposited what she would tell me to, and that was it.

"Really," I said, trying to save what little face I could. "It would be easy. I would stick a couple of thousand in the checking account to cover any outstanding bills until I could figure what bills came in and at what times of the month. Then it would just be a matter of organizing the payments accordingly."

"*Really*," she said. "You think that's all there is to it?"

"Yeah, what else could be involved?"

The ride home was a long one that evening. I had insulted Kathy's ability to competently keep us solvent. But we were both right that night; she, because I really didn't understand the scope of the job she was doing or how difficult and time consuming it was. And me, I was right too, because I did exactly what I said I would do after she died.

So sitting by the table paying bills that night, I thought of Kathy again and asked that she would forgive my insensitivity, but no answer was forthcoming and none was really expected.

Frustrated with insurmountable bills, I picked up the phone and called Jo Anne just on a hunch she might be home and would like to talk. I desperately wanted to hear her voice again. She answered, and I was pleased she recognized my voice. I asked if she had time to talk. It was a little past nine, and I apologized for calling so late.

She seemed a little hesitant. She said she was talking to someone on the phone, and if I wouldn't mind, could she call me back? I gave her my phone number and said to call back anytime no matter how late, I would be up.

The phone rang a few minutes later. It was Jo Anne, a little out of breath.

"Are you all right?" I asked.

"Oh, fine," she said. "I was so excited that you called that I wanted to get back to you as quickly as possible. I ran upstairs so I could have some privacy."

"Well, I really didn't mean for you to cut your other call short," I said.

"Oh, that's okay," she said. "It was just an old friend. I can always call back."

We talked for over an hour, and the time seemed to fly by. I enjoyed our conversation and we made arrangements to talk again later that week. As our relationship would grow, that evening call would become for us a life-line: our way of keeping our sanity and staying in touch whenever our family responsibilities prevented us from seeing each other.

We reluctantly said good night. It was painful to hear the click at the other end of the line.

I lay in bed that night thinking about many things. I thought about how much I would like to see Jo Anne again, about how much I was missing my wife, and oddly enough, about "old friends."

XVII

Later in February of that year the district in which I teach was proposing a school referendum on the upcoming ballot in March. Along with many others, I had done my part in drumming up support for the referendum, and as a final show of appreciation the referendum committee had planned a dance at the local community center. It was to be a big bash, and I had invited Jo Anne to attend. She was at first reluctant as she didn't want anyone from the community looking disparagingly upon me so soon after my wife's death. I assured her that no one would feel that way, but if any one would really be so insensitive, I could deal with it. Besides, I told her that I didn't give a damn how anybody else felt. I wanted her to be my date for the evening. I actually felt very comfortable asking her to attend, and I hoped she did, too.

Jo Anne agreed to go, and I was as excited as a school boy once again. I picked her up around eight. This time I reluctantly shot a round of horse with her son, and, of course, was soundly beaten.

Chris, now feeling the dominant male role had been established, left us alone. We had a drink and talked a little bit about the importance of the referendum. I couldn't take my eyes off her. She was beautiful. I felt a definite excitement about her and I hoped she felt the same about me. She made me feel alive again. and I felt good just being near her.

We left and drove to the party, not really saying very much. I pulled in the parking lot near the back of the facility. I remember telling her that I would park here in case we wanted to leave early. I was looking into her eyes. We were speaking to each other without having said a word, yet we were saying so many things. Nothing really needed to be spoken.

We slowly moved toward each other and our lips met for the very first time. It wasn't at all awkward or forced. Her lips were full and moist, her breath warm and sweet. It was electrifying. I had not kissed another woman this way in over twenty-two years. It had been worth the wait.

We left the car and walked toward the clubhouse. It was very casual, almost automatic, how our hands came together. It felt good again just to hold someone's hand. I was amazed how well our hands fit together. I know I keep saying the same thing, but it is true. I felt like a school boy with his new, best girl. I liked the way I was feeling.

There was a large crowd. The room was filled to capacity with local supporters from the community as well as nearly all our district's teachers in attendance. The music was in full swing, and it seemed people were having a good time. I immediately sensed that people were looking at us as we entered the room, some casually, others more intently. All of them seemed to be aware of my recent circumstances and smiled at us as we walked through the room toward a table. I was very excited to be with Jo Anne, and I guess it showed, because many people would give me that "knowing look." if you know what I mean, as I would introduce her to friends and colleagues.

Everyone seemed to approve that we were together. Not that it would have mattered had they been aghast, but it helps to know that people are supporting you in as many ways as they can, particularly by being nonjudgmental. Besides, I was finding it hard to believe that anyone would not approve of Jo Anne for any reason. She was beautiful, charming, and genuinely sincere. If anything, I was positive people were wondering why she was with me. Frankly, *I* was wondering why she was with me. Whatever the reason though, I was glad she was.

I went to buy her a drink and returned to find her talking to some mutual acquaintances. I placed her drink on the table and asked her if she would like to dance. She excused herself from her conversation and walked with me to the dance floor. The floor was crowded and people were moving to the rhythm of the music. She moved into my arms and we just looked at each other for a moment. We had never danced together before, but it was like we had been dancing together all our lives. She was fluid on the floor and made me appear to be a better dancer than I know myself to be. I remarked how graceful I thought she was. She told me, with a twinkle in her eye, that it must have been because of the years of ballet she had taken as a child.

I asked her if she wouldn't mind my making an observation. She looked at me carefully but didn't say no, so I took that as a yes. "After very close scrutiny," I said, "I have concluded that you are the most beautiful woman in the room tonight."

Now some women might have thought, "Here it comes, the big push, the big come on," yet that was the farthest thing from my mind. I had said and meant it with as much honesty and sincerity as I have ever said anything in my life. I believed her to be absolutely stunning and I was just amazed that she was in my arms at that moment.

She blushed and I could tell she was not use to such flattery. She thanked me with those big blue eyes of hers and I smiled. We finished the dance without saying another word. I walked her back to the table and asked if she would excuse me for a moment; then I left her to finish her conversation.

Some time later that evening the familiar sounds of "Lady in Red" began to pulse through the room. She turned to me, and without saying a word I led her by the hand to the dance floor. There was the music. There was the night. It was as if we were alone, just the two of us, embraced in each others arms and swaying to the sensual rhythms of this passionate song.

I felt totally alone with her, as if we were not on the same plain as anyone else in that room. We were in a different dimension each so in tune with the other that we seemed almost to blend into one. Her fragrance danced about my head and I could not breathe in enough of her.

Our eyes became fixed on the each other. We seemed to occupy the same space as we stood on the floor while all the others whirled about us. I caught a glimpse of one of the teachers smiling in our direction, seeming to know just as I knew that this was special in some mysterious and wonderful way. We were one. It was intoxicating.

As the song regretfully came to an end, we stood transfixed for a moment in each others arms. Our bodies parted and we walked slowly back toward our table.

"It's wonderful," she said, "how that song keeps coming up."

"Yeah," I said. "It was worth every penny."

The party was nearing its end. All the speeches had been given and the cheers were laid to rest. We left before just the crowd would rush for the door. As I pulled into her driveway, she asked if I wouldn't like to come in for a little while. I was still reeling from our dance and did not want the night to end, so I followed her in and we went into the great room. She asked if I would like to have a fire and I nodded yes.

"I don't have a fireplace at my house," I said. "I wish I did."

"We really don't use it much," she said. "I guess it's because I don't have anyone to enjoy it with."

"Would you mind if I made myself a drink?" I asked.

"Not at all, please make one for me, too. Scotch would be fine."

I brought the drinks over to the fireplace and placed them on the hearth. With the fire now under way, Jo Anne and I sat on the carpet in front of the fireplace.

The light from the flames danced on her face and she looked radiant. I couldn't help but look at her.

"What?" she inquired with a smile. "What are you looking at?"

"I'm looking at you," I answered. "You are beautiful."

"Oh please, I look awful. I'm tired and not looking my best."

Sensing I might have said something wrong, I suggested it was late and that maybe I should be leaving. "No, please. I didn't mean for you to leave. It's just that I'm not used to so much attention," she said. "I am truly flattered and just a little embarrassed. This is all so new to me."

"For me, too," I said. "I'm sorry if I embarrassed you. It's just that I find you very attractive."

Just then, a crackling, almost screeching rang through the silence like a shot in the dark. "Jo Anne, is that you? Who's with you? I know someone is there. Jo Anne, is that you?"

"I'm here, Mother. I'm with a friend. I'll be with you in a minute," Jo Anne replied.

I could see a figure hunched in a wheelchair at the entrance to the great room.

It was only a slight step down from the dinning room to the great room floor, but far enough that Millie, in her wheelchair, could not navigate it by herself. This was a barrier that I would come to appreciate nearly as much as Millie would come to despise it.

"I need my back washed," she cried as she wheeled herself back into the darkness of a hallway. "Don't make me wait too long. Tell Richard * I said hello."

"Maybe I should go? " I suggested again.

"No, please. Just stay. I'll only be a few minutes. Please wait till I get back."

"Okay, I'll stay, but only if you're positive," I replied.

"I'm positive. Please make yourself comfortable by the fire. I'll only be a few minutes," she insisted.

With that she left and vanished as quickly as did her mother. Now this vanishing thing was interesting. Jo Anne has this habit of moving so quickly from place to place that she literally seems to disappear. It's the damndest thing. Sometimes I just turn my head when she is standing next to me and when I look back she'll be gone. It's scary when it happens. And it drives me crazy.

I sat on the floor in front of the fireplace and nursed my scotch. I was really feeling more and more unsure about being there, what with her mother needing Jo Anne's help and all, but I was enjoying the fire and was hoping to enjoy more of her company as well. However, there was something else nagging at me.

Jo Anne returned shortly, smelling slightly of liniment. "I'm sorry about all that," she apologized as she re-entered the room. "I usually rub her back down with lotion each night. She has a hard time sleeping when I forget to do that for her."

"I understand," I said. But I was not feeling right. Something was bothering me a little, and I reasoned that I had better say it now before things went any further between us.

* not his real name

"Jo Anne, some time ago I asked if you we were seeing anyone, and you said that you were not. If that is true, who is Richard?"

But before she could even respond, I apologized. "I'm sorry. I don't have a right to ask these questions of you. It's just that if I would have known that you were seeing someone, I would not have asked you out. Really, I should be going," I said.

She sat patiently, and I could sense she was preparing her answer very carefully. "As I recall," she said rather lawyer-like, "you asked me if I was seeing anyone *seriously*, and I told you no. That was then and is now, still the truth."

She let that sink in before she continued. "I have not been seeing this man on a regular basis, but I believe he feels we have a relationship," she explained. "I assure you that I do not perceive it that way at all. I have dated him less and less frequently as time has gone by, and I have never led him to believe that we were more than just good friends or that we were moving toward something of a more permanent nature."

"I just want you to understand, Jo Anne, that I do not interfere with other people's relationships. Maybe you should get this straight with this man before he thinks someone is trying to move in on him," I suggested.

We sat by the fire and really didn't say much more that evening about anything, just small talk really. We certainly did not talk about the "other man" or about her mother either, for that matter. I could tell that Jo Anne was upset that the evening was ending a lot differently than she had intended. That's when I recognized that lives aren't quite so neat and clean as we would like them to be. We have obligations and commitments that strap and bind us in this life, and when we try to put new lives together, it can become a nearly monumental task.

This man, Richard, would present a minor setback to us as

Jo Anne and I tried to formulate our own relationship. Jo Anne's relationship with him was, at best, one of convenience. Both of them were lonely and in need of comfort, but he had work-related and family obligations from which he could not remove himself even after his own divorce was final.

As it turned out, I knew the man personally and found him to be an honorable man whose heart was always with his estranged family. He was a person who, when finally faced with the realization that Jo Anne and I loved each other, was man enough to step back and give Jo Anne and me the space we needed without any further interruption.

I was appreciative of that and admired his resolve to let us be. He still is a friend of Jo Anne's and I respect that friendship and all that it entails. I go to sleep each night comfortable in our love, and I never concern myself with her past. We have each other, and that is all that matters.

I often wondered if I could live with the knowledge that my spouse had a relationship(s) with another before we married. I now know that to dwell on such things is destructive and unproductive. A past relationship is not a breach of commitment. It is not a betrayal. It is just one more of life's experiences that we draw from as we struggle to find the meaning in all this.

Life seems to me now to be all too short to allow these types of negative thoughts to permeate a good and loving relationship. We all have needs as people, and we seek refuge where we can, even with people we know with whom we would not spend the rest of our lives. Past relationships do not make anyone less a person nor have they made our love any less valid.

I believe learning to love again means learning to recognize love for what it is, at any age when it occurs. It is the one thing that we are capable of feeling all our lives with as much passion, perhaps even more, as when we were young. In fact, it makes one young again. When I see my students falling in love (albeit puppy love) I don't just try to remember how they feel, I **know** what they are feeling. It is senses heightened to acuteness beyond description. It is the resurgence of euphoria once thought lost in the past. It excites people around you, and even makes them a little envious of this new found joy. And I am sure it also rekindles the once warmed embers of long ago in the hearts of many who are still receptive to one of life's finest gifts. Love -- ain't it grand?

As I prepared to leave that night, I asked Jo Anne if she would like to attend a dinner and play. I thought it would be a good idea if she met some friends of mine. She said yes and I was excited to be going with her.

Another date and we still hadn't had our first fight. This was getting good.

XVIII

The dinner and the play was a test of sorts. I was introducing Jo Anne to friends Kathy and I had been close with for over twenty years. I was curious as to how they would feel about her, but I also wanted them appreciate how much I enjoyed her company. I was also, I am sure, looking for their acceptance of this new "relationship." As strongly as I was feeling about Jo Anne, I wanted other people, close friends and eventually family, to understand that this was not some rebound thing or think that I was dating some "bimbo" to fill a void in order to satisfy a need for sexual gratification (although that thought had crossed my mind.)

The evening went well for the most part. I think all of us were under a little strain. Jo Anne knew full well she was being compared to Kathy. They, I'm sure, didn't really want to scrutinize her, but couldn't help doing so, as would everyone who had known Kathy. It was inevitable, predictable, and unavoidable.

Both Jo Anne and I felt that my female friend was a bit standoffish and cool toward Jo Anne that evening, and I knew she was having a hard time accepting this new person in an old role. But Jo Anne and I still managed to hold hands and look at each other with that look that told the world there was something special between us, something neither Jo Anne nor I had much control over. On the other hand, my friend's husband was comfortable with Jo Anne and seemed to enjoy her company. Since that time, these friends have unfortunately divorced and are dealing with a different loss, but a loss all the same. Both still remain close friends with us. She and Jo Anne have come to understand each other very well, and have become good friends. All our lives have become richer for it.

Later that night I would take Jo Anne home. As we sat on her couch, we held each other and didn't really talk much. I kissed her forehead, her cheek, and then her mouth with a long and meaningful kiss. Her lips responded with as tender and warm a kiss as I had ever received. We just melted into each others being and the kiss seemed never to end.

I held her face in my hands and I wanted to tell her so many things, but I was afraid to say anything at that point. I could see confusion and fear in her eyes. Later she would tell me how frightened she had been about my vulnerability. Imagine that; she was concerned about not taking advantage of me.

I was just plain afraid. I was afraid I was losing control, that I was betraying a lost love, that I might be pushing her too fast, and that I was going too fast. It was all very confusing, this new relationship thing, and it was frustrating both of us.

We cooled down a little and talked about the evening and how it had gone. I discussed my friendship and the history I had with our dinner companions. Our families had been together for many years and then mostly because of geography and job related responsibilities, we had drifted apart. Somehow, I started talking about how we had our children so early in our marriages and how expensive and costly it had become to raise them. Jo Anne agreed.

I think that is why I said the next thing. In some convoluted way, I was trying to tell Jo Anne that it was tough raising children these days, and I was not up to it anymore or more correctly, that future offspring were not in my future plans.

"Jo Anne, there is something I need to tell you." I paused and said, "I've had a vasectomy." The silence was deafening. I couldn't believe I had said it. Just like that. I was such a jerk. Not only was it incredibly presumptuous, but it reeked of male perversion. I hoped she wouldn't be too offended by my stupidity or my testosterone laden remark.

"Ah! A vasectomy!" she exclaimed. "Really?"

I thought all was lost. I was sure she thought that all I was thinking about was sex. What else could she have thought? What other options had I left her? I wouldn't have blamed her if she had thrown me out on my dumb ass. Needless to say, the mood had changed again. My chagrin must have been as obvious as the stupidity of my remark. After a few uncomfortable moments we both just laughed, she at my clumsiness and I at my inanity or maybe it was the other way around.

But she didn't throw me out, so there was still hope left in Muddville. The mighty Casey hadn't yet struck out or maybe better stated he hadn't yet been ejected from the game.

XIX

As our relationship progressed, we would try to meet as often as possible. Stealing minutes from our daily routines just to be with each other became a challenge. I have to admit that Jo Anne was much more creative at than I was. We often met at the nearby forest preserve for a quick lunch, or I would rush over after work for just a few minutes to say hello. But where our relationship really developed and intensified was on the phone late at night.

After her son and mother and my daughter had gone to bed I would call Jo Anne and we would often speak late into the evening. Our conversations seemed to fly by. It was a time for us to really get to know each other. It was an opportunity for me to understand Jo Anne's life and what she faced every day, as both her son and mother would vie for her attention, neither of them giving much back in return.

It was a time for me to avoid the loneliness of the night, which I had come to dread. Night was the worst time for me. My sons were away at college and my daughter was involved with school and was generally in bed by 10 p.m. That left me alone with the night. These phone conversations with Jo Anne saved my life. They were so important to both of us that missing a nightly call was almost like going through withdrawal. Our conversations, I believe, helped cement our feelings. It was like we had known each other for years and understood each other so well.

Sometimes these calls were early enough in the evening that my daughter could not use the phone, and some resentment was developing. I didn't often indulge my children, but I was learning to pick my battles, and this was a minor issue that could have developed into a major catastrophe. The solution was easy. Within days my daughter had her own phone line and peace was at hand.

On occasion, our discussions would lead to flirtatious little conversations. They were often titillating, and indirectly they were on a level that opened the door to sex.

It is important to note here that Jo Anne was much more mature about this than I was. She was fully aware of the relatively short time lapse between Kathy's death and the onset of our new relationship. Jo Anne was ever vigilant of its evolution and mindful of my psychological state. She had been here before; she knew how fragile a relationship like this can be and just how fragile I was at the time. She understood all of this, but me, I was just horny. And she understood that, too.

So making love was inevitable, but it would be on her time table, not mine. It could also come with a price. We were both adults, so I thought I understood all the ramifications that it would entail. Personally, it was a huge step for me. I had made love to only one woman in the last twenty-three years. There is a certain familiarity and comfort level that goes along with that, and there is also a certain complacency that accompanies life-long mates. That is not to say that love making when married is not a wonderful experience, but only rather that it is safe. Very little risk-taking or spontaneity exists as families and lifestyles take their toll on relationships, especially sexual ones. As children get older, the parent's sexual encounters inevitably decrease or at the very least are worked around the children's schedules rather than one's own passions.

Then one day in early spring, while Jo Anne and I were together enjoying an after dinner drink, she had very calmly and in an unassuming way told me that her blood tests had all come back negative. Now sometimes I can be pretty dumb, but not this time.

"Ah!" I said. "Your blood tests were negative. Really!" I smiled. She smiled. And now I got just a little bit scared. Sometimes you have to be careful about what you ask for in this life. I now knew Jo Anne was ready, but was I?

In any event, now that I had to put up or shut up, I made arrangements to have the use of a relative's condominium in the heart of Chicago's Gold Coast. That evening was cool and clear and the view from the 34th floor was spectacular with the city sprawled out beneath our feet. This was a night that I, and I hoped she, had looked forward to. But I knew we were both very apprehensive.

I had so many doubts about that evening that I almost backed out at the last minute. I admit that I was scared, very scared. I was having a hard time dealing with the guilt and unfaithfulness I was feeling. I was wondering if she would find me attractive, and if I measured up to her expectations. At the same time, Jo Anne was having her own doubts. We were like two adolescents fumbling about, trembling even, as their first sexual experience was about to occur; not sure what to expect but ever so eager to find out.

As I lay in bed with this woman for the very first time, I looked deeply into her eyes. She held me in her arms, fully aware of my pain, cradling me as a mother would her child, and I knew she understood. I cried, and she wept with me. We were both paying the price. I knew it would come to this if we were to share this new reality. I wasn't cheating on my wife. That would have been an easier thing to do. A man only really cheats on a woman he doesn't respect or love. This felt more like a betrayal.

Jo Anne understood this, too, and she also knew she might be held responsible for that betrayal if I was not the man she hoped I was. She understood that this whole thing could backfire and the relationship could end as quickly as it had started if I had been too eager, if I was not really ready. She knew that she could be held responsible. The once nightly phone calls might continue for a while with less frequency, and then they would stop altogether. This would be the price we would pay if I was not ready. She had to choose the time, and she had to be confident in her judgment of me and of herself. The timing had to be perfect.

Virginity is lost only once, but there can be new levels of awareness that become open to you, levels you never knew existed or had long since forgotten. That night we, were reminded once again of the power and beauty of that singular human experience we call "making love". Our spirits were once again raised as we came to appreciate being alive and the sharing of our most intimate humanity.

The next morning I awakened before Jo Anne and went into the kitchen to make some coffee. I went back to the bedroom and sat in a chair alongside the bed so I would not disturb her. She looked so peaceful lying there. She was beautiful in the early morning light, and I was glad that I was there with her. She stirred in the bed and slowly opened her eyes. She smiled and said good morning. "Why are you sitting there? "She asked.

"I'm keeping watch," I said with a smile. She closed her eyes and returned to sleep, safe in the thought that I was shielding her from worldly demons.

I hadn't realized how much I had missed that feeling of protecting some one I loved. Maybe it's just a male thing. I don't really know. But it felt good to be watching over someone I cared about again. I liked it and it made Jo Anne feel more comfortable, too. It's what a man does when he loves someone. It was then that it occurred to me that maybe I was falling in love.

XX

We had survived our first lovemaking experience despite a jealous friend, a despotic mother (who had only just begun to fight), and a son who was still unsure of his place in all this. Now it was time for Jo Anne to meet my family. Not only my children, but also my parents and the scrutiny of my brothers and sisters, all six of them had made it their duty to ensure that no lady was going to take advantage of their brother at a time when he was surely at his weakest.

This was especially true with one of my brothers, Tony, and his wife. It was a delicate situation for many reasons. My brother Tony is my identical twin. We have never spoken in any special "twin language," nor have we ever had any nefarious telepathic, or any telepathic communications for that matter, yet our relationship is undeniably close.

Barbara, his wife, was a life-long friend. She and Kathy had gone to both grammar and high school together. Tony and Barbara's story closely paralleled that of mine and Kathy's in so many details they are too numerous to mention. These were the two people who would most closely examine this new relationship, and neither would hesitate to tell me their observations. Those opinions in themselves would not cause me to stop seeing Jo Anne if they believed her to be in any way "not my type," but I admit I would have weighed any objections carefully. It was important for me to have them like Jo Anne as

I was sure I was going to spending a lot of time with her. If they found her as wonderful as I had, they would soon spread the word to the rest of the family, which would relieve some of the pressure on me of going through this process with each and everyone of them individually.

I called my brother and asked if he and Barbara were free on a Friday night, and as fate would have it, they were. I told him I was bringing someone over for them to meet and that we would be there around 7:30 p.m. Of course, he asked me who this person was and what she was like. I described her as well as I could, trying not to seem like an enamored young school boy hopelessly in love, which of course, was exactly how I was feeling.

"Tall," I said. "She's tall, slender and very attractive."

"And?" he asked.

"And what?" I responded.

"You know," he said.

Well, actually I didn't know. "Her name is Jo Anne. She is Slovak, I think," I said that because when you're Italian, family members want to know that sort of thing.

"Ah, a Slovak woman!" he exclaimed.

"What the hell is that suppose to mean?" I asked.

"I don't know," he retorted, "you brought it up."

"I'll see you later," I said. And with that I hung up. I knew they would be very anxious to meet Jo Anne. I just hoped Jo Anne was ready for them.

On the way over that night I explained to Jo Anne that I was a twin, actually a mirror twin. I am right-handed, he is left-handed, that kind of thing. I asked if she was nervous. She said that she was, just a little, and asked what Tony was like. "You mean besides looking like me?" I teased.

She smiled at my feeble joke. I went on to describe both of Tony and Barb as best I could, complimenting them in every

74

way I knew how. I especially told Jo Anne how supportive they both had been since Kathy's death. I did caution her about Tony's sense of humor but assured her that Barb would not let him go too far with it this first night.

"Just be yourself," I said. "They'll like you. Who wouldn't?"

Jo Anne didn't appear quite as confident as I did, but that is her nature. I parked the car, and as we walked across the street to their house, and up the stairs towards their front door, I asked her if she was sure about this. Without responding verbally, she reached over and rang the door bell.

After we nervously survived the formal introductions, we all sat down, and just made casual conversation. The evening was a huge success, as both Tony and Barb made Jo Anne feel very comfortable and welcome. They could sense that we were drawn to each other and drew from the other a certain strength.

Some time later that night, my niece came home and I introduced her to Jo Anne. Janet was polite but a bit curt. I was a bit surprised by her behavior, but Jo Anne quietly asked me to let it pass. She already understood what I was to discover later, that my niece was very upset to see me with another woman. Many months afterward Janet would tell me that as hard as she tried to hate Jo Anne, she just could not. "Jo Anne," as she would say, "was just too damned nice to hate."

We finished our visit, and I drove Jo Anne home. I stayed for a while but soon left as Jo Anne was being beckoned to perform her nightly duties, both as mother and daughter. After I arrived home I called my brother and asked him what he thought about Jo Anne. Tony and Barb had both agreed that Jo Anne was a wonderful person and it was very obvious that we cared a great deal for each other.

"Was it all that obvious?" I asked.

"That Slovak woman's got you, brother," he said. "Just don't rush into anything too quickly."

"Thanks, Dad," I said with a hint of sarcasm. "I'll try to behave myself."

Then Barb got on the phone and told me how nice she thought Jo Anne was and how obvious it was that we were fond of each other.

"That obvious, huh?" I asked again.

"Oh, yeah!" she exclaimed. "But that's fine. You deserve to have some happiness again. Just don't rush into anything."

"Thanks, Mom. What is this a parent's convention?" I joked. "But thanks, Barb, I really do appreciate your opinion. This was a difficult night for me and Jo Anne."

"And for us, too," she admitted. And I had agreed. How could it have been anything less for them?

I slept well that night, perhaps better that I had in a long time. The next day I got a call from my mother. "When are we going to meet Jo Anne?" she asked. "Tony and Barb say she is very nice. Why not bring her over for dinner on Sunday?"

"Wow! That was fast," I thought to myself. The news had spread even faster than I imagined it would.

"Well, I really don't know what Jo Anne's plans are for the weekend, but if she is not too busy, I'll ask her."

"Good," my mother said. "I'll wait to hear from you. I love you."

"I love you too, Mom." I hung up the phone and wondered when it would all end. It was only just beginning and already my head was spinning.

XXI

Somehow we had avoided the trip to my folks' house that weekend, but it was time for Jo Anne to meet my children. On this rare occasion, all of them were to be home that weekend. Mike and Jeff would be home on spring break, and Michelle, still in high school, was home as usual.

I told them one evening that I was bringing someone home for dinner that week and would appreciate them all being home to share it with us. I was planning my best dish, spaghetti with homemade red sauce and meatballs, Italian salad with garlic bread, and some apple pie for desert. They all knew something was up when the big dinner was planned. This was obviously important to me, and they sensed it and played along as I went raving around the house like a madman, making sure everything was just right.

"Take it easy, Dad," Mike stated. "Who is this lady anyway?"

That was the key question: Who was this lady who I was bringing home to meet my children? Well, it was simple, I thought, she is a friend. Someone who helped bring me back from the brink of despair and opened her hand and her heart to me.

I wanted my children to meet this remarkable individual who was helping me put my life back together. I wanted them to see Jo Anne as I did, but I was so wrapped up hoping they liked her that I often would not allow them to formulate their own opinions.

This was especially true of Michelle. My daughter had become so important to me after her mother's death that I wanted and needed her to really like Jo Anne. I knew there was no way Jo Anne would be able to take Kathy's place in Michelle's eyes, but I wanted them to develop a genuine and warm relationship.

I had heard terrible stories about how Daddy's little girl could make the new significant other's life a living hell. I truly didn't believe this possible of Michelle, but I just didn't know.

I did know, however, how sensitive Jo Anne was, and I didn't want her to feel slighted in any way. More often than not I would embarrass Michelle by saying really stupid things to her in Jo Anne's presence such as; "Michelle, aren't you going to say hello to Jo Anne?" or "Michelle, don't you think Jo Anne's dress is pretty?" or God knows what else. It was terrible. One night Michelle confided in me how hard it was to accept Jo Anne in my life, not for any other reason but for the fact Jo Anne was not her mother. She knew how important Jo Anne was becoming in my life, and she was happy for the two of us, but she pleaded, "Please, don't treat me as if I were a child. Let Jo Anne and me accept each other on our own terms, not on your insistence."

It was, of course, perfect advice, and also the same advice Jo Anne had given to me on numerous occasions herself. I had a lot to learn about building relationships between families. I was also learning something about my daughter. She was maturing much faster than I had given her credit for. It was becoming ever clearer to me how many different ways Kathy's death had affected us all.

In any event, the first dinner went well. They learned a little bit about the mystery woman, and Jo Anne came to understand a little more about them and me. Later that night, Jo Anne was to remark how nice it was to meet my family and to appreciate how important family was to me. I tried to explain to her that ever since I could remember, I had been taught there were only four things that really meant anything in our lives: one's faith, self, health, and family. Without these, a man would be very poor indeed. A simplistic view of life, perhaps, but the older I get, the more important those four things become to me. If my father was to leave us nothing but those words, they alone would be a legacy worth cherishing.

In the days and weeks to follow, Jo Anne and I would struggle with finding time to nurture this new relationship. It would involve careful planning; time and circumstances would prevail upon us to have a great deal of perseverance and patience. I was still very actively involved in our high school's booster club, in Michelle's life, and in my own teaching and coaching. Additionally, Jo Anne's son Chris was a bit immature for his age and very dependent on her for the attention he desired. Jo Anne's mother was also becoming increasingly suspicious of my motives and jealous of the attention Jo Anne was showering my way.

Jo Anne had really been responsible for her mother in many ways from the time she was about sixteen. Except for the first year of her first marriage, Jo Anne had lived with her mother all the years of her life.

At first Millie was pleasant and cordial, but as time went on she became more and more distant . On many occasions when I would come over, Jo Anne would greet me at the door and Millie would ask, "Who's that at the door? I can't see you."

"Hello, Millie," I would say. "It's Pete."

"Oh," she would say, "it's you," and not say any more.

It also became increasingly obvious how her Millie's maladies would become more painful and require more attention when I would visit. It was something about which Jo Anne was often embarrassed, but we both understood her mother. We hoped that someday she would see how much Jo Anne and I meant to each other and come to accept our feelings and perhaps, even, give us her blessing. That dream never would come true, and it bothers Jo Anne to this day that her mother had so little interest in her happiness.

Millie, suffering from advanced arthritis and other problems, would command huge quantities of time from nearly everyone. But her needs always seemed to escalate when either Chris or I would have need of Jo Anne. I believe Millie saw me as the devil incarnate come to take her very soul away. She saw in me someone who would so captivate her daughter that there would be no time left for her. As it came to pass, Millie's health would erode to such a point that Jo Anne would be unable to take care of her and still keep her son, work, and home afloat, let alone our relationship. In time, a decision would need to be made.

Whatever Jo Anne would decide, I would support her in that decision. But Jo Anne came to understand that she, in the end, would have little choice. It would become an easier but nonetheless painful decision for her as the relationship between Millie and Chris would so deteriorate that Jo Anne felt it was in her son's best interest to place his grandmother in a convalescent home. That decision would send dramatic ripples through her family that to this day have not been fully addressed, but it probably is for the best.

In time, as is common for many people placed in convalescent homes, Millie would resist all help and refuse her medication. In less than a year after entering what she would perceive as internment, Millie's heart, fatigued from the strain of disease and age, would simply stop beating. Both she and Jo Anne would finally get some rest.

XXII

It was late on a Friday night in May. Chris was spending the night at a friend's home, as was Michelle. Jo Anne and I had just returned from dinner, and we sat on the couch trying to relax from the week's strife. I was very content. I was thinking about how nice it was to have Jo Anne next to me, and I realized how important she had become in my life. I looked at Jo Anne and she smiled. I gathered up as much courage as I could and said, "Jo Anne, I think I am falling in love with you."

There, I had said it. I think I knew it all along, but I was reluctant to admit it, fearful she might laugh or run away. I immediately could see mixed feelings on her face. She hadn't responded to my proclamation and I thought that I had offended her. Here I was in the middle of this new and exciting relationship, and I go and try to ruin a good thing by saying something, as the old song goes, stupid like "I love you."

"I'm sorry," I said. "I didn't mean to upset you. It's just that I think about you all the time. I want to be with you and I hate it when we are apart. I feel good when I am near you, and I think you feel the same. I want to spend as much time as I can with you. And if that's not love , then I'm not sure what it is."

"We need more time," she said. "I need more time, and I want you to be very, very sure. You need to think this through, and I need to give you the time to be sure."

Well, once again Jo Anne proved to be the consummate politician. She hadn't said she didn't love me, and she hadn't rejected my declaration either. I felt better about that and considered it a victory of sorts.

Even after Millie's death Jo Anne and I would still have to steal time during the day to see each other. Often times I would run over to her house during my lunch break just to see her that day. The few minutes we would have together would be enough to get me through to the next day. As it was becoming increasingly more difficult to spend time together, Jo Anne and we would steal every possible minute we had on the weekends. It frequently meant me staying at her house or her at mine for a night, or worse, staying very late and then driving 45 minutes back home.

Staying over for the night meant one of us would have to leave our children at home alone. It could be argued that my daughter was certainly old enough to left alone, yet I was not comfortable with the idea. I would suggest Michelle spend the night at a friend's, but you can burden others only so often, and besides, Michelle was more comfortable at home. Jo Anne's son, on the other hand, was not quite old enough at thirteen to spend too much time alone, so more often than not I would stay at her house. If we were to spend any time together, it would have to be that way. Jo Anne would come to my house periodically, but it was just better if I made the trip.

Regardless of where the time was spent, it was spent getting to know each other. We were acutely aware that we had no history together. It became obviously painful when we would be with the others family and friends; one of us would feel sort of left out in the cold. We couldn't relate to so many circumstances. We would desperately try to make the other feel comfortable during these times, but it didn't always work. It was especially hard for Jo Anne. My circle of friends was a bit larger, as was my family, and all of them had their own history intermingled with Kathy and me. But Jo Anne and I were creating our own history, and because of that, we became more selfish with our time. We both knew that my daughter and her son were a little bit resentful of this. To their credit they understood this in their own ways and gave us as much room as they could and still lay claim to us as parents.

Establishing a history is not an easy thing to do. It requires a great deal of patience and understanding. We were on the road to starting a new life together, but first we needed to know and understand where the other had been. Beside the love and passion of a new relationship, we felt there was a need for something more substantial, some basis for understanding the other. Perhaps that is why so many marriages fail these days. People fail to build a relationship on their understanding of the other. Who is this person I am about to commit myself to? Once the bells and fireworks are over, who am I sitting across the kitchen table from? Commitment is a term that has nearly lost all meaning in so many relationships today. It's just plain easier to get divorced than it is to struggle through some difficulties to make a marriage work.

Neither Jo Anne nor I were ready to embark upon this journey without being comfortable in our understanding of the other before any commitment was made by either of us.

Our first year and a half together had ended. It had full of pain and growth; excitement and discovery. It was a beginning where I had only been faced with endings. I believe it was fate that brought us together. Our destinies had crossed, and as destiny so often does, it presents opportunities to those who see beyond the apparent. Very few people ever really get a second chance at anything in this life, let alone a second chance at love. I was ready to write a new history, and I needed and wanted Jo Anne's help.

XXIII

Eventually all the people we were close to, family and friends, had the opportunity to meet Jo Anne or me. We were becoming an item, and people could see that we were more than just friends. It is hard to hide genuine feelings of warmth. Neither of us are particularly fond of exaggerated public displays of affection. We would hold hands, and be sure we didn't lose sight of the other in a crowd, but other than that we were a bit too old for the smooching and cuddling in front of others routine. But it was clear to all with eyes that we were seriously interested in each other.

We would spend every possible and practical minute available to us together.

Jo Anne was especially creative in planning many of our meetings. Sometimes she would often call me at school, leaving a message to meet her for lunch at a local forest preserve. With lunch already prepared, we would talk and discuss the day and often our next possible meeting. It was fun and exciting, planning when and where we might meet again. I would often stop over after school ended and spend an hour or so with her and with each passing day my feelings for her increased. I was falling more and more in love with her and I believed she with me. However, only I had confessed such feelings openly. She was still a bit skittish, but I could feel she loved me, too.

Since it was not always easy to see one another, we would connect via the phone. We found it increasingly more difficult to say goodnight. I wanted and needed her near me. Many times our conversations would help stave off a panic attack as I lay in my bed alone, afraid and without companion or counsel. We supported each other in our efforts to keep our families together and our sanity intact. I would often find myself aching for both the woman I had lost and for the woman whom I had found and with whom I so desperately wanted to share time.

After one lengthy evening phone conversation I again told Jo Anne that I loved her. This was not one of those "I think I love you" statements. It was just "I love you."

There was a deafening silence on the other end of the line. I waited for a response but there was none. "Jo Anne?" I asked, "Are you still there?"

I could hear some muffled noises and finally she said, "Yes, I'm here. I'm just crying because I love you, too."

"I'm sorry; did you say that you loved me, too?"

"Yes, I do," she said. "I have for awhile. It was just that I wanted to be sure about all of this. I just didn't believe it could happen to me, and I wanted to be sure you were sure. But yes, I love you so very much."

Oh man, the feelings that went flying through me were incredible. I was on a roller-coaster riding through a kaleidoscope of emotions. I was excited and fanciful, elated and melancholy; young again but feeling a terrible burden, but most of all I was amazed and just plain happy. I remember telling Jo Anne that I didn't know what I had done to deserve two wonderful women in my life, but that I would be forever thankful that she was in mine, and that I would never betray her love.

"It's funny," I said. "Just before I called you tonight I was about to shut off the radio and the Beatles were playing. Guess what tune they were singing?"

"I have no idea," she said.

"'She Loves You', of course," I said. "It was prophetic."

"Yeah! Yeah! Yeah!" she sang, and we both laughed. I liked her sense of humor.

"Goodnight, Jo Anne," I said. "I love you."

"Goodnight, Pete. I love you, too. I really do."

"I know," I said. As I hung up the phone I became suddenly and acutely aware of the significance of the last few moments.

Her phone rang only once. "Are you sure?" I asked.

"I am very sure. Scared, but sure," she said.

I hung up the phone.

"Oh, brother," I remember thinking, "What do I do now?" I fell asleep thinking of old loves and of new loves; of one life ending and a new one beginning; of sugar and spice and everything nice; and of old Beatles tunes.

"Yeah! Yeah! Yeah! With a love like that, you know you should be glad."

XXIV

A tremendous burden had been lifted from my shoulders as I came to appreciate that Jo Anne loved me. I had been so fearful that our relationship would just fade away after a couple of dates and that I would be forced to join the singles crowd once again. I don't think I would have managed that very well. I'm sure friends would have introduced me to many of their single friends, but that was very frightening to me. It would be more likely that I would have just stayed pretty much alone and let the chips fall where they may. But now all of this was moot. I had found a woman who loved me, and it felt wonderful.

Being in love is a very powerful experience, especially the second time around. I was older, much older than the first time, and so I thought I was experienced in life and its inconsistencies. But I was not prepared for the power of this feeling of rebirth and the excitement of being alive again. I began writing again, and every poem was for or about Jo Anne. She occupied my thoughts nearly every free minute, and I became intoxicated with her. My senses were heightened around her. I could smell her scent, sense her touch, and feel her presence from across a room.

Often times we would be at a social gathering and would find ourselves separated by a sea of people. I would sense she was looking for me, or she would sense the same about me, and we would visually search the room for the other. We would then lock eyes and our total concentration would just be centered on each other.

Ever so imperceptibly, I would slightly raise my head to let her know that I loved her, and she would do the same, and we would smile and go back to our conversations. To this day we still communicate in this way just to let the other know that we are as one, that we are special in our love.

I felt that we were connected in so many different ways. And the best part was that she felt the same way. People around us knew that we were in love. It was interesting to observe others observe us. I would often sense many different emotions coming from the same people. Sometimes I would sense people had an inner happiness that was genuine for our new-found joy, yet simultaneously, there were feelings of regret that we had each lost someone in our lives. However, the response from everyone we knew was overwhelmingly one of delight that Jo Anne and I had found each other and that we were in love.

I also noticed how being around two people who genuinely love each other often causes others to appreciate their own relationships all the more. Simply by our obvious attraction, our friends and relatives seemed to rekindle their own loves. At least they did for a while. Eventually, for those who fail to completely understand the power of love, complacency creeps back in and things often return to where they once were. But for a short time, anyway, people became a bit closer because of our love. If nothing else, it offered hope to those who thought of love as only a fleeting thing.

It was great to be in love again. I cannot express the rejuvenation one acquires as the full impact of being in love unfurls. Flowers smelled sweeter, the air was fresher, and life had new meaning. However, it is easy to get wrapped up in the "loving to be in love" experience. We were both aware of this and took each day as it came, relishing every moment together and learning from the other. As cautious as one tries to be in love, we would always move forward as intelligently as our past experiences and years would allow. But Lord, it was a delightful whirlwind.

Before we knew it, it was the holiday season once again, and we were rapidly approaching the beginning of our second year together.

That year's holiday season was even better in the sense that the grief over my loss was still very real, but it was less painful. One evening, as the holidays were approaching I asked my daughter to sit beside me on the couch. I reminded her how proud I was of her and how understanding she had been concerning my relationship with Jo Anne and how I still loved her mother so very much. But I explained to her how important Jo Anne was to me and how strong my feelings for her had become. I reached into my pocket and handed her a small box. She opened it slowly and hugged me, telling me how happy she was for me. She said the ring was beautiful and she felt sure Jo Anne would love it. I wanted Michelle, above all others to be the first to know of my intentions. I felt she deserved at least that much. Later she and I discussed a thousand things: possible wedding dates, where we might live, all those types of possibilities. Of course I didn't have any specific answers for her because I didn't know if Jo Anne would even accept my proposal. But I did make her one promise, and it was that I would not get married or move from our home until she had finished high school. After that, anything was possible.

We both cried a little bit and laughed a little bit, too. She asked me when I was going to propose to Jo Anne, and I told her I had planned to do it on the anniversary of our first date at the very same Chinese restaurant. I was excited and anxious for that day to arrive.

The holidays came, and I sent Jo Anne pink poinsettias once again with a card signed, "Thinking of you." Nothing else needed to be said.

XXV

It was a wonderful holiday season. There still remained a certain emptiness that could not be ignored, but time was healing the painful wounds, or at least soothing them enough so that despair was not part of the picture. This was now our second Christmas together, and Jo Anne and I enjoyed it like no other in recent memory. I was preparing for something I had never thought I would do again: ask another woman to marry me. It was something I had never even considered, yet, there I was, making plans to ask this beautiful woman to marry me, not really sure what her answer would be. But I think I was pretty sure. I remember thinking to myself that no one with any understanding of women at all (not that I am claiming to be any more understanding than the average guy) would buy a ring and ask someone to marry him if he wasn't pretty darn sure that she would say yes. Nobody normally sets themselves up for rejection. So I was pretty sure she would say yes. I wasn't sure **why** necessarily, but at least I hoped it was because she loved me as much as I loved her.

January 30th came and my plans were all set. I picked Jo Anne up later that evening and we proceeded to the restaurant. It was a chilly night, and I was hoping the restaurant would be as slow that evening as it had been on our first date. But it wasn't, and I was a bit perturbed that there were really no private tables available. We were seated next to four older business types who were a little loud and apparently glued to their chairs; I thought they would never leave.

Jo Anne asked me more than once during dinner what was troubling me, as I seemed to be preoccupied. She had no idea what thoughts were running through my mind. All I wanted was for the people next to our table to leave. She even asked me why I kept looking over at that table with a slightly disgusted look on my face.

"Was it that obvious?" I thought to myself. I just wanted those people to leave. By the grace of God and all the vibes I sent their way, they finally got up and left.

"Jo Anne," I said, "what do you think about the last two years. I mean, about you and me?" I didn't have any idea why I asked that question other than just to give myself more time to muster up the courage to propose.

I don't even recall her answer. I just remember reaching into my pocket and handing her the ring box. "This is for you, Jo Anne."

She took the box in her hand and just sort of stared at it for an endless second then, with what I perceived as a trembling hand, she opened it ever so slightly.

I was holding my breath as she gazed in astonishment at the sparkling diamond. "Jo Anne," I said, "I love you and would be greatly honored if you were to become my wife. Will you marry me?"

"The ring, it's so beautiful! And I am just so shocked!" she exclaimed.

Now I was starting to get nervous. "Well, is that a yes?" I asked.

"Oh yes, it's a yes. I would be very proud to be your wife," she said. "I love you very much. Are you sure this is what you want?"

"Jo Anne," I answered, "I have never been more sure of anything in my life."

I took the ring from the box and slid it on her finger. I looked deeply into her eyes, held her hand, and told her once again of my love for her. She smiled. We were embarking on this new trip and we were excited about the journey, but we didn't know exactly where it would take us. We just knew we would be going together.

Older now and wiser, yet no less in love than on our first ventures, we had come to this point in our relationship with an ease that would offer us a greater understanding of love, marriage, and all the responsibilities and possibilities that lie within.

We picked up our things and left the restaurant a lot warmer than we had entered, wrapped in the love of a bright future and secure in the memories of the past.

The night ended with a fireside glass of champagne, and we shared the excitement with her son, who would later tell his mother how happy he was for her and wished her luck.

I kissed Jo Anne goodnight and told her I would call her when I got home. The drive home was a long one for me that night. I was thinking of many things, and of Kathy in particular. I remembered all the things I had said to her about loving her forever and being true to her. I felt as if I was betraying her and our love. I thought about the vows we had spoken so many years ago. About how we had pledged our love to each other and how we would love each other until "death do us part." But you see that's not how I always perceived it. It was like we were bonded together forever. Isn't that how it is supposed to be? Isn't that the way it is in all our stories of undying love, in all our love songs, in all our dreams?

This has been perhaps the hardest thing for me to accept these past years since Kathy's death. We get this notion that we will spend not only this life with a spouse, but also the next. Who will I spend eternity with?

In a monogamous world, can there be a polygamist afterlife? Perhaps we are only meant to aid and comfort the other here on this earth; such things may not be necessary in the world beyond. I am sure I worry myself needlessly, and, I worry less often these days. I have learned that I cannot answer such questions, so I now leave these unanswerable dilemmas in God's hands. I just look forward to every day with Jo Anne because she brings joy to my life and a comfort to every day.

It is safe to say that I have no control beyond the here and now. That is what I have come to understand. It is acceptable to love another woman after a spouse has died or after a divorce. Loss is loss, regardless of the nature of it, and we are bound to find true love where ever it may be. If it should present itself to us and we fail to grab hold with both hands for fear of tarnishing a previous love, then love and life will pass us by, and in so doing death (or loss) will have claimed another victim. I choose not to surrender to those pressures until my last breath has been spent, for life is too precious to live without love.

I have come to understand that loving another after the loss of a spouse is not a betrayal of the earlier love. It is easy to say that the deceased loved one would have wanted it that way, but it is not the deceased loved one dealing with the guilt. I need to remind myself periodically that it is okay for me to love, with all my heart, a person who deserves my love because she in turn loves me.

I've met some people who have told me that they will never love another as much as they love first spouse. That may be true. But to say you could never love another because there is no room in your heart is a denial of your right to happiness. Does loving another demean a previous love? Life is too short to ponder such unanswerable questions, but still they are hard to avoid. I believe all of us who go through these experiences, have these questions to deal with, and that is normal too. I also believe we are obligated to live out our lives as happily as possible with those we love and who love us. Love is one of the few experiences that separate us from our neighboring species. Why not accept it as a true characteristic of our humanity and let it happen? To rejoice in love is to rejoice in life.

XXVI

Each of us, when we enter a new relationship brings along some "baggage" with us, for lack of a better term. These are the millstones of life we acquire that tend to drag us down and inhibit us in our new relationships. They might be children; parents; family or friends; past occurrences. They are the burdens that we must bear, and in so doing, they threaten the development of new relationships.

Jo Anne and I both had to deal with such problems in order to establish a solid footing for what we hoped would be a sound foundation in this relationship we wished to develop. First, we had to deal with guilt. Guilt in its ugliest form can destroy a relationship before it ever has a chance to begin. You must be above the ploys of others who try to chip away your attempts at happiness for the sake of their own selfish needs. When two different families come together, there is always some stress that will take place; ours would be no different. Jo Anne's stepchildren from her first marriage were on their own now and supportive of us. They were older and really had little at stake regarding any of Jo Anne's decisions. My two sons, who were away at school for the most part and so removed from our developing relationship, could have chosen to be negative. Instead, they were supportive from the start. That left two people whom we felt would be the hardest to deal with, my daughter and Jo Anne's son.

Having gone through this once before, Jo Anne was not about to be accepted as anything other than who she was, the woman I loved. She opened her heart to us all and hoped she would be accepted for herself.

In the mean time, I was trying to be accepted by Chris as a friend as well as be respected as a father. As I perceived things, I saw Jo Anne struggling with a son who was by all appearances a spoiled young man. The conflict between grandmother and grandson had placed Jo Anne in the middle for so many years that it was easier to appease her son with gifts than to change the views of his grandmother. Jo Anne, in trying to be both mother and father to a demanding young boy, acquiesced to many demands in his life that still present problems today.

One day, when Chris was being less than cooperative with Jo Anne, and demonstrating a little power struggle on my behalf, I took him aside and told him that regardless of his behavior, I still loved his mother and that I was not going to just go away. Nothing he could do was going to change that. He looked at me kind of funny and went to his room, and although he didn't become totally supportive overnight, he did seem to understand that we were not going to let him interfere with our happiness.

To his credit he did tell his mother, some days later, that he was glad she was happy and that he liked me. That was some improvement, and things have been getting better ever since.

Chris has grown up a lot since those early days, but he still has some way to go. He often does not understand family and family responsibilities. He still believes his needs are more important than anyone else's and has many misplaced priorities. In his defense, so do many people his age. More often than not it is my impatience with him that causes some undo friction. We are both getting better at this step father/stepson routine. There are limits to my authority, and there are limits to my patience. We are each learning to respect the other, and that is making life easier for us all, especially Jo Anne.

It is hard to deal with children from a previous marriage. You have certain expectations that were part of your previous family life, and now, just by the nature of your being, they become a part of some one else's. Right or wrong, these expectations are real and hard to let go of. This can and often does lead to many problems with step children and with the new spouse.

I felt if these expectations were good enough for my children, why weren't they good enough for my stepson? Ultimately, one is forced to face the fact that one's expectations are just that, expectations, not edicts written in stone. With patience and understanding you will come to understand that the other children, just like yours, are each different and expectations may need to be readdressed.

Jo Anne's son had very little direct influence from anyone. Chris's father had died when Chris was only 10 years old. It became survival time for his mother, and she received little support from anyone in the process. His half brothers and sister were older and had lives of their own. Their attempts at influencing him in a constructive direction were well-intentioned but too far and few between to offer any real guidance. Forced to seek help elsewhere, Jo Anne turned to the Big Brothers/Big Sisters organization for help in offering Chris a positive male role model and someone he could talk to.

This was a good decision for Jo Anne and a worthwhile experience for Chris. His "Big Brother" understood his role well and became a good friend to all of us. I came to know Jerry as a concerned and caring man who had, I believe, the proper perspective with Chris. We had many conversations with the "big brother" and would often discuss the direction Chris was taking. But as my involvement became increasingly more prevalent, and as Chris grew older, his "Big" would soon depart as is the design of the program. Jerry still calls periodically and he and Chris share lunch together on occasion. He will be a friend of this new family for a very long time, and we are appreciative of his efforts and the efforts of that organization.

One spring evening, Jo Anne and Jerry asked if I would like to attend the annual Big Brothers/Big Sisters Dinner and Awards program. I went for many reasons, but mostly I was curious as to how this whole system worked. The program was typical of so many community organizations: speeches, awards given to the hard working few who do it all, chicken served buffet style, all in a room that was so overcrowded you wondered why you had come at all. Then, when you could barely tolerate another speech, a question was posed to the audience. This question was not addressed to everyone in attendance, but rather to a very special group of people. The children themselves were asked if they would like to express their appreciation to their "Big" for their help and support throughout the year.

Slowly, one by one, the kids moved forward to the podium. They were lined up, boys and girls from the ages of 7 to 16. They came in all different shapes, sizes, and colors. Some were in wheelchairs, others were on crutches, hair tussled in every direction. Some were smiling, some looked scared to death. But none of them, not a single one, was forced to go up to the front. It was purely voluntary.

As the children in their own special ways thanked their "Big" for their aid and support, you could not help but be moved by the genuine expression of love each child conveyed so uniquely and profoundly. I recall that one young boy came to the podium and simply cried. Not from fear, but because he was so moved by the special relationship he had developed with his "Big", who himself was just some average man who found time in his day to help a child in need. The boy could not find the words to adequately say thank you. None needed to be spoken.

It was a fitting tribute to the adults who help these younger children. There was not a dry eye in the room as child after child spoke a few words so eloquently about their feelings. All the while I kept turning to Chris, looking, expecting him to get up and thank his "Big," but it didn't happen. I know his mother was disappointed, as was I. But if Jerry had been disappointed, he never gave a hint in that direction. He cried and laughed with us and I think he knew what was in Chris' heart even if Chris didn't publicly state it. Showing emotion can be a scary thing to anyone, especially a young boy who had lost a father, was getting a new one, and who didn't yet know who *he* was.

There are many people in our lifetimes that deserve thanks, some whose impact may be so subtly profound that the power of it may not be known for years. Yet, it is the hope of his mother and me that Chris thanks his "Big" someday in a way that truly will be reflective of his feelings.

XXVII

Meeting family and all that entails should not be looked upon as a necessary evil. I have a large family: six brothers and sisters, numerous cousins, aunts and uncles, nieces and nephews all who wanted to get a look at this lady who had come into my life and about whom they had heard just a very little. And I also wanted her to meet my first wife's family, the in-laws. I thought it was important for her and them to meet each other as we would be meeting for birthdays and such. It was important to me that they continue to include my family in their future, just as it was important for me to include them in the future activities of my family.

Kathy's death had a terrible and immediate impact on her parents. Kathy's mother had relied a great deal on Kathy's support. They would often talk on the phone and we would visit them frequently after Kathy's father had retired. I have known her folks nearly all my life as there is a relationship through marriage that brought our families together.

Kathy's father is a retired postal worker who is an intelligent man, well-read and current with world events. He was also a stubborn man who rarely saw another's point of view. Oddly enough, as we both got older, he came around to my way of thinking, or   was it that I was just catching up with his? But that is neither here nor there. Through the years I have come to know, respect, and love my father-in-law. Those days surrounding Kathy's death introduced me to a man I had never seen before. Perhaps, if it were possible, her father was in as much pain as I was. His grief was intense. He had suffered a heart attack some years earlier and understood the fine line between life and death. He searched his heart and soul for a reason that would explain this tragedy. He even went so far as to think an incident at his daughter's birth may have been the ultimate cause of her death.

He recalled at birth she needed help for her head to crown properly, so forceps were then used to assist in her delivery. He thought perhaps that was the cause of the aneurism. I did my best to assure him that it was not likely, but I had no real idea, and did not wish to discuss it at that time. I did my best to divert his grief away from some event that neither he not I had any control over, but he was lost in his own inexorable suffering. Perhaps the hardest thing for both him and his wife to accept was that a child should die before the parent. That's not supposed to be how it works.

Kathy's mother, Jean, was a mild mannered lady of the old school. Her job was to take care of her husband and family, to provide meals and keep a tidy house. She was a woman who performed her duties well and who loved her children as mothers do. She kept herself on the outside of any discussions and always let her husband do the talking. She rarely, if ever, interfered in the marriages of her children, and in all the years had known her, I had never heard her say a negative word about anyone or use a vulgarity in any way. Jean's own mother, who had died some ten years earlier, lived with them until the end, and Jean had seen her mother slowly lose her mind and her life to Alzheimer's disease. Jean possessed an under riding fear that she would experience the same fate. She always had it in the back of her mind that Kathy would be there to help her and her father if Jean became unable to cope.

This was Jean's ace in the hole. But as she had gotten older, bouts of forgetfulness, more than that which we all experience from time to time, were occurring on a regular basis. Her husband, in his denial would blame it on her medication. Kathy knew better and was fearful that the worst was yet to come. Of course, we thought we had time, but then time ran out. Kathy died, and Jean has since left this world of the present to live in a world only she could see and hear and understand.

Alzheimer's would sap her strength and inevitably her life away just as it did her mother before her. I am thankful, at least, that Kathy never lived long enough to see her mother destroyed by a disease that erases a life time of memories.

I was not surprised however, that both her parents readily accepted Jo Anne into their lives. They opened their hearts to her and made her feel welcome in their family. Kathy's brother and sister, their spouses and children have all opened their arms to Jo Anne and have always made us feel welcome in their homes. They continued to include us in many of their family celebrations and we tried to make as many of theirs as we could. Both Jo Anne and I are indebted to their generosity and continued support.

Meeting Joe and Shirley Mae, well, that was a whole other story.

XXVIII

Meet my parents, Joe and Shirley Mae: a second generation Italian-American, Catholic male married to a third generation Norwegian-American Lutheran female. Seven children, eighteen grandchildren, six great grandchildren and many more to come, I am sure, and they were still married for over fifty years. My father, a bread man working twelve to fourteen hours a day, midnight to two in the afternoon six days a week. The reality of it all astounds us to this day: how did they procreate such a large family?

Basically my parents raised two separate families. First, there were the "boys": myself, my twin Tony, and two younger brothers Bruce and David. Then there were the "girls"; Marianne, Carol and Katherine. We "boys" always referred to this duality as those days when the old man was shooting straight, and those when he was shooting blanks. But that's a family joke.

In any event, Jo Anne, this new lady of my dreams, would have to meet my parents and all the brothers and sisters. This was a bit overwhelming for her, so we did this in segments; first my twin brother and his wife, then it was Mom and Dad's turn. I knew they were both very interested and anxious to meet her especially after Jo Anne had already met my Tony and Barbara.

Now my father just wanted to meet this "Mogee" as he called her, an Italian name for "lamb eaters" or Croatians. My mother, on the other hand, wanted to make sure this lady was in my best interests, of course. Mom would never tell me not to see Jo Anne again, or that she was not good enough for me; instead, she would just ask me if I was planning on bringing *her*, or would *she* be coming to such and such. But it was time, so dinner was arranged and I had to prepare Jo Anne once again.

As nervous as Jo Anne and I were at this meeting, the dinner went very smoothly. When my mother could determine for herself that Jo Anne was not some money-seeking widow who would toss my life into ruin, the four of us have never been closer. I came to realize that even at my age my parents were still concerned with my happiness. When they saw that I was truly happy, they accepted Jo Anne into their hearts as if they had known her all their lives.

Jo Anne, having lost her father at an early age and her mother just a year after meeting my folks, was eager to accept my parents as her own, and the four of us have shared many wonderful days together. Jo Anne made it a point to call my parents often, to plan outings we could go on together, and to just share time together as often as possible.

Had my parents, or family and friends for that matter, made Jo Anne's presence in my life difficult I don't know what may have happened. I like to think I was of strong enough character to have persisted in my relationship with a person who I believed loved me regardless of the pressures placed upon us. Fortunately the support group around me and Jo Anne loved us enough to see that we did in fact love each other. This time love would win out.

XXIX

Engaged now, pondering the future became a nightly ritual for Jo Anne and me. Staying true to my word, I assured my daughter that we would not move until after her graduation, so where to live was the question on everyone's mind. I loved the community where I lived. I knew so many people there and was actively involved in the school community, but I knew my home could not accommodate a larger family. And in all fairness to Jo Anne's son, why should he be forced to give up his friends and school when Michelle hadn't?

We considered buying a new home free of the past offering a fresh start for everyone. But with two offspring already in college, one to begin a year later and one more a year after that, and with the cost of houses sky rocketing, it didn't seem financially prudent to purchase a new home. It became apparent that Jo Anne's house was the only practical solution. With some renovations it would be large enough to accommodate all of us, and it was centrally located for everyone's needs. It was the best solution.

When it was possible we had every one meet at the "new" house. A tour was given to my kids as Jo Anne and I explained what plans we intended to make in order to accommodate the "family." There was a very large bedroom we would make into two bedrooms. My sons, who were rarely ever home, would share the newly constructed bedroom, while Jo Anne's son would have the other half, which included his own bathroom. Since we were essentially invading his space, we felt it only fair that he keep the bathroom. My daughter would be given Millie's old room, and she had a bath right across the hall.

Jo Anne and I would occupy the area above the garage which would be perfect for us. With that decided, we debated the time of arrival. It would be after Michelle's graduation, but before she entered college in the fall. It didn't take long for people to figure out that meant we would be moving in before Jo Anne and I were actually married. I don't think any of us knew what that would entail.

Sharing living quarters prior to marriage was something new for my family. Being engaged made it more palatable for some, but I knew it didn't sit well with my parents, especially my mother. They never really said anything, but I knew they were not totally comfortable with it. And I have to admit I was concerned how it would affect all the kids, and I wondered how it would affect me if, for some unforeseen reason the marriage did not take place. I was the one who moved. I was the one who had sold his home in order for this to occur. I was the one, if the bottom fell out, left with nowhere to go. I expressed these sentiments to Jo Anne, she fully understood my apprehension.

She suggested that we see an attorney and have the deed to her house changed so that we would both have our names on that document. I was appreciative and relieved. This woman was so in tune to what needed to be done that I would be a total fool not to marry her. I was praying I wouldn't do something stupid to cause her to change her mind about me.

Our engagement would last for nearly a year and a half, but the time flew by.

We decided we would have a simple but elegant garden wedding at "our" home. Jo Anne and I thought it would be nice if she asked Michelle to be her maid of honor and I ask Chris to be my best man, thus symbolizing the unity of our two families. They both agreed and were excited about it.

At last the arrangements were made and finalized. The house and yard looked beautiful. We had a tent set up in the back yard with a small chapel near a grouping of spruce trees. About one hundred of our family and closest friends were in attendance that day as Jo Anne, escorted by her brother, walked down the flower-adorned aisle. Kathy's parents, brother and sister graciously attended the ceremony as well.

Father Tom, the very priest who presided over Kathy's funeral service, would now be joining me and Jo Anne in holy matrimony. Every song selected to be played or sung had a special meaning to us. We hoped that people would be listening to the words, but what really mattered was that Jo Anne and I would be listening.

A little rain had moved in the morning of the wedding, perhaps a tear or two from a previous love, a reminder of loves past and tears of happiness for the loves ahead. But the sun would not be denied on this day, and as Jo Anne walked down the aisle, every head was turned to view this beautiful lady who so deserved this happiness.

She was stunning and graceful. Once again swept away by her elegance, I wondered what it was I had done to deserve this person in my life. Later we would dance to "You Take My Breathe Away," and oh my, had she done that.

We joined hands and turned to listen to the words that would join us as husband and wife. Each of us, first me then Jo Anne, repeated vows that would guarantee our love and devotion for the remaining days of our lives. Tears of sadness for the end of one marriage and tears of joy for the beginning of another flooded the eyes of nearly everyone present. As the ceremony came to an end, my son, Jeffrey, moved by the emotion of the moment, suddenly came up and hugged us both. Then my son Michael, then Chris and Michelle each embraced Jo Anne and me. I have never been so moved. The genuine expression of love at that moment was overwhelming.

Later that night, when nearly all the guests had left, Jo Anne and I, along with our children, sat by the fire pit, enjoying the glow that radiated about us. I was once again reminded of the power of love and whatever the struggle, love was worth every risk, every hardship.

Elated, I jumped up and danced around the fire and howled at the moon. Jo Anne laughed, and the fire sparkled in her eyes. We had learned to love again.

Epilogue

My daughter was particularly interested in two pieces of jewelry that had belonged to her mother. One was Kathy's diamond engagement ring. The other was a silver-blue pearl that Kathy had actually found in an oyster on a trip she had made to the east coast. Michelle hinted that she would like to have these items, especially the pearl, but I had told her that I thought the pearl to be lost.

Upon her graduation from college I presented my daughter with this poem and a small package.

On Your Graduation

Through all these years,
struggling with loss and
the need to grow,
you have become the woman
your father admires
and the one your mother
dreamt of so long ago.

But, sometimes even death
cannot take from us
those treasures from the past
that bring us ever closer
to those whose spirit
lives within us all,
and whose maternal love still lasts.

Michelle slowly opened the small box and cried as she placed the ring upon her finger. Surrounded by two small diamonds was the silver-blue pearl she had thought was gone forever. I was so proud of my daughter. My only regret was that her mother would not know the wonderful young woman our daughter had become, or the fine young men our sons had become as well.

Nearly two years later I would present Michelle with one more gift from her mother. On the day of her wedding shower, I asked if she would like a gift from me. She looked puzzled but nodded yes. I handed her another small box and told her that I loved her and hoped she would wear this on her wedding day. Inside the box was her mother's engagement diamond I had reset in a necklace. On her wedding day my daughter asked me to place it around her neck. It was one of the proudest moments of my life. We both cried a little, and then went on to enjoy a most wonderful wedding.

Afterword

Since the beginning of our adventure together and the work on this book began, our marriage has been tested in many ways. In one year all three of my children were married. Talk about a strain. But it all worked out, in spite of my occasional rantings and ravings about the cost. Yet, once again, Jo Anne came to my rescue, as she would always find a way to "cool my jets," as she says. Since then, six beautiful grandchildren have entered this world with whom we share our love.

But tragedy also found its way into our lives as my younger sister and my mother would both pass away within two years of each other.

Jo Anne's son would also find himself in trouble, as so many of our young people do these days, and this perhaps has been our greatest struggle. That in itself is a whole other story, but it appears to be headed toward a positive conclusion. Let me say that if our love had been the least bit tentative, our marriage may not have survived this latest trial. As Kathy had always been the stronger one, so it is with Jo Anne. The struggle continues. Our love endures.

Printed in the United States
22783LVS00001B/145-273